D0689355

Dr. Ann's

Eat Right for Life®

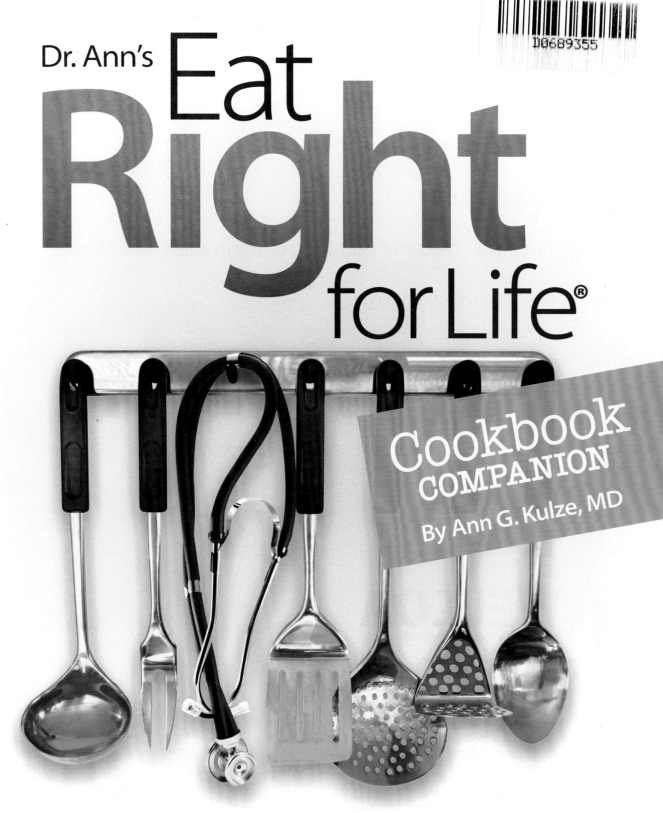

Cookbook COMPANION

By Ann G. Kulze, MD

Editorial Staff

Author: Ann G. Kulze, MD

Executive Editor: David Hunnicutt, PhD

Managing Editor: Brittanie Leffelman, MS

Contributing Editors: Madeline Jahn, MOL, Elizabeth Kulze, Carie Maguire

Multimedia Designer: Adam Paige

WELCOA
your premier resource for worksite wellness

17002 Marcy Street, Suite 140 | Omaha, NE 68118
PH: 402-827-3590 | FX: 402-827-3594 | welcoa.org

©**2013 Dr. Ann G. Kulze (Written Content)**
©**2013 Wellness Council of America (Design & Layout)**
Information may not be reproduced, copied, cited, or circulated
in any printed or electronic form without written permission
from the publisher.

Dr. Ann
Ann Kulze, M.D.

Ann Kulze, MD
CEO
1 Pitt Street
Charleston, SC 29401
PH: 843.329.1238
www.DrAnnwellness.com

Table of Contents

About WELCOA

The Wellness Council of America (WELCOA) was established as a national not-for-profit organization in the mid 1980s through the efforts of a number of forward-thinking business and health leaders. Drawing on the vision originally set forth by William Kizer, Sr., Chairman Emeritus of Central States Indemnity, and WELCOA founding Directors that included Dr. Louis Sullivan, former Secretary of Health and Human Services, and Warren Buffett, Chairman of Berkshire Hathaway, WELCOA has helped influence the face of workplace wellness in the U.S.

Today, WELCOA has become one of the most respected resources for workplace wellness in America. With a membership in excess of 5,000 organizations, WELCOA is dedicated to improving the health and well-being of all working Americans. Located in America's heartland, WELCOA makes its national headquarters in one of America's healthiest business communities—Omaha, Nebraska.

Check out Dr. Ann's entire nutrition series at WELCOA's eStore:
http://www.welcoa.org/store/

About **Ann G. Kulze, MD**

Ann G. Kulze, MD is a renowned authority and motivational speaker on nutrition, healthy living, and disease prevention. She received her undergraduate degree in Food Science and Human Nutrition from Clemson University and her medical degree from the Medical University of South Carolina, where she graduated as the Valedictorian of her class. With formal training in both nutrition and medicine, in addition to her extensive "hands on" experience as a wife, mother of four, and trusted family physician, she has distinguished herself as a one-of-a-kind "real world" nutrition and wellness expert. She is the founder and CEO of the wellness education firm, Just Wellness LLC, and author of several books including the award winning, best-selling *Eat Right for Life®* series.

When she's not writing, researching, or motivating others through her speaking engagements, Dr. Ann lives her wellness message in her native Charleston, SC where she enjoys swimming, running, kayaking, cooking, gardening and spending time with her wonderful family. Learn more at **www.DrAnnWellness.com**.

From Dr. Hunnicutt

About Dr. David HUNNICUTT

Since his arrival at WELCOA in 1995, David Hunnicutt, PhD has developed countless publications that have been widely adopted in businesses and organizations throughout North America. Known for his ability to make complex issues easier to understand, David has a proven track-record of publishing health and wellness material that helps employees lead healthier lifestyles. David travels extensively advocating better health practices and radically different thinking in organizations of all kinds.

A mountain of information extolling the benefits of healthy eating has been handed down through the ages. Whether it's feeling better, performing at a higher level, or living longer, there's little question that consuming healthy food is a cornerstone of good health. Because of the overwhelming evidence supporting better nutritional practices, physicians and nutritionists alike are urging Americans to make important lifestyle changes that involve healthier eating.

Unfortunately for the common person—because of time constraints, tight budgets and limited knowledge—putting essential nutrition information into practice is virtually impossible. In our fast-paced, push-and-shove world, there are just too many barriers that keep us from eating the foods that are most nourishing and nutrient-rich.

Until now!

With great excitement, I am pleased to announce the release of Dr. Ann Kulze's *Eat Right For Life®: Cookbook Companion*. In this ultrapractical cookbook, you'll find a broad assortment of healthy recipes for every meal and snacking desire. What's more, the ingredients in the recipes are not only good for you, but they're affordable, they're filling and, perhaps most importantly, they'll improve your health.

Beautifully illustrated, Dr. Ann's cookbook offers a wide array of simple meal suggestions for breakfast, lunch and dinner—and each recipe comes complete with ingredients and helpful preparation instructions. Again, if followed, the advice and recipes in this book will help you eat healthier, feel and look better, and live longer.

We owe a great debt of gratitude to Dr. Ann Kulze for making this cookbook a reality. As one of the nation's most progressive physicians, Dr. Ann has an uncanny knack of making complicated things simple to understand—and that's worth its weight in gold when it comes to eating better. In this beautiful book, Dr. Ann takes you by the hand and shows you exactly what to buy and how to prepare it as she shares the recipes that she personally uses to keep her family healthy and well. And because these are Dr. Ann's personal recipes, she's worked through all of the important details that will make your quest to eat healthier much easier.

We hope that you enjoy Dr. Ann's *Eat Right For Life®: Cookbook Companion*— it's one of the very best cookbooks of its kind.

Warmest Regards,

D. Hunnicutt

David Hunnicutt, PhD
CEO
Wellness Council of America

Cook **Right** For Life

This book is dedicated to the wonderful reality that preparing healthy meals can be simple, easy and delicious. As a working woman, devoted wife, and mother of four, I relish the hour when the day is done, and I can enter the wholesome haven of my kitchen to prepare the family meal. Some of you may shudder at the idea of the kitchen as a refuge, or meal preparation as anything close to an enjoyable experience, but this book promises to calm your fears and arm you with the right apron for quick, healthy, no-sweat cooking.

In the pages that follow, I share with you my favorite recipes from 20 years of family meal experience, including all the best tips, tricks, and strategies I have picked up along the way. All you need is a sharp chopping knife, colander, large and medium sized pot, large skillet, can opener, and a little motivation! Thankfully, due to recent studies that family meals improve the health and well-being of both parents and their children, this fading tradition is now on the upswing, and this book is here to celebrate it! Cooking for oneself and one's family is a healthier, leaner, cheaper, and far more positive way to live.

This book will also shatter the myth that cooking tasty and nutritious meals is a difficult feat. In your hands, are the recipes for 10 dinners, (including side dishes) eight lunches and breakfasts, and four desserts, and most of these can be prepared in as little as five to 30 minutes! When was the last time you spent less than 30 minutes at a restaurant or waiting for a delivery? Yes, cooking your own meals can actually save you time!

With a busy family that has a large appetite, delicious and healthy meals have always been a centerpiece at my kitchen table, and as my husband and children will attest, all of the recipes that follow will delectably silence any growling stomach! As hard-working, loving parents, we want the best for our families, and ourselves, and this should include good health. Knowing that every ingredient in these meals is 100% wholesome and nutritious, preparing them will be a labor of love. Think of this recipe collection as the hands-on, "take me all of the way" companion to my book, *Eat Right For Life®*. It is your step-by-step roadmap to healthy and tasty eating and an inspirational tool for maintaining optimal nutrition. I encourage you to read both and place them where they belong: on your kitchen counter. Let them serve as a reminder that delicious and healthy meal preparation is just an arms-length away. Let's get cooking!

—Ann G. Kulze, MD

Eat **Right** For Breakfast

A healthy breakfast is the most important ingredient to an energized and productive day. People who regularly eat breakfast function better mentally and physically, and enjoy greater success in maintaining a healthy body weight. Eating breakfast primes your metabolic pump and aids in appetite control throughout the remainder of the day. Because many traditional breakfast foods are amongst the most wholesome and nutrient dense, breakfast provides a fantastic opportunity to consume more of the 42-plus essential nutrients our bodies require to function at peak capacity. And if you adhere to the breakfast guidance that follows, you can lower your risk of cardiovascular disease, type 2 diabetes, obesity and metabolic syndrome, and possibly improve your health by lunchtime!

To fully leverage all that breakfast has to offer, make sure you include at least one food from each of the following three categories at your breakfast:

1. **A healthy protein.** Nuts, nut butters, seeds, soy milk, 1% or skim milk, low-fat yogurt, reduced fat cheeses, smoked or canned salmon, omega-3 eggs, low-fat cottage cheese, high protein cereals, and protein powders (for smoothies) are convenient protein options.

2. **Fresh produce.** Fruits, especially brightly colored varieties like berries, citrus, red grapes, cantaloupe, kiwi, apples, plums and mango are wonderful breakfast options. But don't forget that fresh spinach, bell peppers, onions and tomatoes are a delicious addition to any egg or omelet dish.

3. **Whole grains.** High fiber cereals and oatmeal are my top-rated whole grain breakfast foods. Additional healthy choices include 100% whole grain bagels, English muffins, tortillas, toast, and granola bars. Be sure they are ***100%*** whole grain or whole wheat!

Here are plenty of delicious choices that fit the bill, so no excuses!

[WHAT'S RIGHT FOR BREAKFAST]

Steel Cut Oatmeal
with Apples and Cinnamon

NUMBER OF SERVINGS
1
NUMBER OF SERVINGS

A warm bowl of oatmeal is a great way to start the day on a healthy note (especially in the winter!). This wholesome whole grain dish provides just the right amount of slow release carbs to fuel your muscles and brain through the morning. It also offers a healthy dose of protein, minerals, and B vitamins, along with a special type of cholesterol-lowering fiber called beta-glucan. If you "dress it up" with a bit of nuts, fruit and super-healthy extras like wheat germ and canned pumpkin, you can take this dish's taste and nutritional fire power to a whole new level of WOW. I am always looking for tasty ways to take advantage of canned pumpkin's unrivaled levels of health-boosting carotenoids and this is one of the easiest ways I have come up with.

Here is how you make this meal…

Ingredients

¾ cup prepared steel cut oatmeal

2 heaping tbsp of 100% canned pumpkin (Libby's® is an excellent brand)

1 oz (about 1 small handful) of pecans, walnuts or nut of choice, chopped

A liberal dash or two of cinnamon

1 tbsp of toasted wheat germ or ground flax

2 tsp of molasses, honey, maple syrup or dark brown sugar

1 small to medium diced apple with skin (about ½ cup) or fruit of choice

Directions

Prepare the steel cut oatmeal in water according to package instructions. Place in a bowl with the remaining ingredients and stir until thoroughly combined.

Dr. Ann's NOTES

➤ Standard steel cut oats definitely take longer to cook (30 minutes), but are the healthiest and tastiest form of oats. Also known as coarse-cut or Irish oats, this "gourmet" oat is less physically processed than rolled or instant oats. This translates to a slower rise in blood sugar levels, which is better for your health and your metabolism. And you'll love their nutty taste and heartier texture!

➤ To save time, you can cook a big pot and store the portions in individual Ziploc® containers in the fridge for up to five days. Some stores now offer quick cooking (five minutes) steel cut oats (Quaker Oats®, McCann's®). These are great options, if available.

➤ Old Fashioned rolled oats are fine, too. Be sure to avoid packaged, flavored oatmeal, as it is loaded with added sugar.

➤ If you want to kick up the protein a notch (which can help with appetite control) blend in two dollops of plain non-fat Greek-style yogurt.

Oatmeal & Fiber: Give Your Body A Boost!

The Importance Of Boosting
YOUR FIBER INTAKE

Unfortunately, the standard American diet (SAD for short) is woefully deficient in fiber. Fiber is an indigestible form of plant-carbohydrate that promotes gastrointestinal health, aides in healthy body weight and reduces the risk of cardiovascular disease. The average American consumes about 12 grams daily—while studies show intakes of 30 or more grams are optimal. Medical anthropologists report that our hunter-gatherer, Paleolithic ancestors consumed massive amounts (up to 100 grams/day) of fiber because of their dependence on the dietary staples of the times which were namely leafy greens, legumes, nuts, berries, roots and seeds. You could say that our robust requirement for fiber is "built into our genes" thanks to our Paleolithic forefathers' diets. Here are some tips for boosting your fiber intake:

➤ **Consume as many fruits and veggies as possible**—the superstars for fiber content include: berries (raspberries are number one), snow peas, apples, canned tomato products, pumpkin, cauliflower, avocado, spinach, asparagus, broccoli, carrots, Brussels sprouts, sweet potato, okra and winter squash.

➤ **Eat more beans**—beans provide more fiber than any other food (up to three to four times more than many fruits and veggies). All beans are fiber superstars, so eat what you enjoy the most. Don't forget about bean dips like hummus, which are delicious! Strive for one serving of beans daily.

➤ **Incorporate a high fiber cereal into your breakfast repertoire**—a good high fiber cereal will have at least five grams of fiber per serving. There are at least 25 varieties/brands now available that fit the bill. One of my favorite breakfasts includes: 1 cup mixed fruit (7 grams of fiber), ½ cup high fiber cereal (5 grams of fiber), ½ cup plain yogurt (2 grams of fiber) and 2 tablespoons of wheat germ (2 grams of fiber).

➤ **Replace refined breads and crackers with 100 percent whole grain versions**—many brands are now available. Check out the newer 100% whole grain crackers on the standard grocer shelf—Multigrain Wheat Thins®, Triscuits®, Ak-Mak®, and Kashi® Heart to Heart®.

➤ **Choose multi grain pasta.** I love the taste of Barilla Plus®.

➤ **Enjoy physically intact whole grains** like barley, quinoa, and brown rice regularly.

Going Nuts: Maximizing Your Oatmeal

Kitchen Tips
NUTS & SEEDS

➤ Roast your own. This is the healthiest, tastiest, and most economical way to enjoy roasted nuts. Simply buy bulk raw nuts/seeds (almonds, pumpkin seeds, walnuts, pecans, etc.), spread them in a single layer on a baking sheet, spray with a thin layer of canola oil pan spray, salt as desired, then bake at 350 degrees until the nuts turn golden or slightly brown (about five minutes).

➤ Store your bulk nuts (raw or roasted) in an airtight container in the freezer to minimize oxidation of their healthy oils.

➤ To lower the sodium content of store bought salted nuts, dump nuts in a colander, shake vigorously over the sink for a minute or two, and place back in the container. This removes excess salt.

➤ Of course, nuts and seeds are great for you raw, too.

[WHAT'S RIGHT FOR BREAKFAST]

Veggie Omelet Scramble

NUMBER OF SERVINGS

1

NUMBER OF SERVINGS

This is my preferred Saturday morning breakfast and it always keeps me full for at least four hours. Given the liberal dose of hunger-fighting protein provided by the eggs and all the "filling" fiber provided by the veggies, it is no wonder that I have to remind myself to eat when lunchtime rolls around! Aside from its delicious taste, this dish is spectacular because it provides three full servings of veggies before lunch!

Here is how you make this meal…

Ingredients

½ medium yellow or red onion, thinly sliced

1 tbsp extra virgin olive oil

2 packed handfuls of washed, fresh baby spinach leaves (about 2 cups) or 1 cup thawed frozen spinach

2 omega-3 eggs

⅓ cup fresh salsa (I prefer Garden Fresh Gourmet®)

Salt and pepper to taste

Directions

In a skillet over low to medium heat, sauté the onions in the olive oil until they are soft and translucent. Add the spinach leaves and stir until they are wilted (about 2–3 minutes). Add the eggs (I crack them right in) and scramble with the veggies until the eggs are cooked to your liking. Salt and pepper to taste. Place the veggie omelet scramble on a serving plate and top with fresh salsa.

Dr. Ann's NOTES

➤ Like most recipes throughout this book, feel free to substitute or add any veggies that you prefer. Bell pepper strips, broccoli florets, diced asparagus, chopped tomatoes, and sliced mushrooms are wonderful options.

➤ Chopped, fresh or dried parsley, cilantro, dill or garlic can provide additional flavor and healthy goodness too.

➤ If you want to add a bit of cheese, go for it. Feta, goat, Parmesan or those made from 2% milk are the healthiest choices.

Veggies Give Your Omelet Incredible Bulk

Kitchen Tips:
VEGETABLES

➤ Make sure you wash or rinse your fresh vegetables thoroughly to reduce exposure to pesticides and harmful bacteria.

➤ Add vegetables to every dish possible to improve its nutritional value. For example, I always add fresh garlic, onions, peppers, and mushrooms to my ground turkey breast spaghetti sauce.

➤ Salads are a delicious and convenient way to get your recommended five daily servings of vegetables. Use as many vegetables as possible in your salads. Ready-to-use bagged salad greens are a healthy and convenient option.

➤ Fresh garlic and onions are great flavor enhancers and contain potent phytochemicals; use them daily in your cooking.

➤ The healthiest way to cook vegetables is to steam, stir steam, bake, or roast them. Boiling or cooking vegetables in a microwave reduces their nutritional value.

➤ Any type of roasted vegetable is delicious. Moreover, when you roast vegetables they shrink in size, so it's easy to get several servings in one sitting. When I roast broccoli for my family (four children and two adults) I use three bundles; when I steam it, one bundle is usually enough.

➤ Roasting is a fantastic way to use week-old produce that you might not otherwise eat.

➤ Soups and stews provide a great vehicle for getting more vegetables into your diet. Try making soup once a week on your day off, and save some for your lunches later in the week. No matter what the recipe calls for, put all of your leftover vegetables in the pot.

➤ Having an appetizer of fresh, cut up vegetables like carrots, bell peppers and celery with mustard, oil and vinegar, or hummus is a great habit to develop. You will likely eat less of your main dish and have greater success in achieving your target of five daily servings of veggies.

➤ Enhance the flavor of your vegetables with some trans fat-free margarine spread, olive oil, lemon juice, vinegar, garlic chilli sauce or any variety of hot sauce.

Continued on next page…

Kitchen Tips:
VEGETABLES *(Continued)*

➤ Washed, pre-cut, bagged vegetables are a great time saver.

➤ Salad greens, cucumbers, radishes, garlic, and onions are most nutritious when served raw (although garlic and onions retain plenty of their nutritional value even when cooked).

➤ Serve cruciferous vegetables and fresh spinach raw or lightly cooked to get the most nutritional benefit.

➤ Tomatoes, beans, peas, and mushrooms are healthiest when cooked.

➤ Celery, chives, scallions, asparagus, peppers, and squash are equally nutritious either cooked or raw.

➤ Season foods with fresh herbs and spices as often as you can as they offer extremely potent concentrations of powerful phytochemicals.

➤ Frequent your local farmer's market. It is a wholesome, fun activity for the entire family, supports the local economy, decreases your potential exposure to pesticides, and offers produce that is tastier, fresher and generally cheaper.

➤ Plant a garden! If you do not have room for a garden, pots or containers will work beautifully for any fresh herb, beets, sweet potatoes, carrots, and lettuces.

Salsa: The Ultimate Omelet Condiment!

Superstar Foods:
SALSA

Thanks to the tomatoes, peppers, onions, garlic, and cilantro that comprise this zesty, great-for-you concoction, salsa is delicious, refreshing, low in calories, and teeming with a synergy of beneficial compounds. It is chock full of vitamin C, potassium, and lycopene along with hundreds of disease-busting phytochemicals. Freshly prepared salsas available in the refrigerated section of your grocery store are the tastiest and healthiest.

[WHAT'S RIGHT FOR BREAKFAST]

Dr. Ann's Favorite Breakfast Smoothie

NUMBER OF SERVINGS
1
NUMBER OF SERVINGS

Smoothies are delicious, portable and if made with the right ingredients, exploding with nutritional firepower. The blending process involved in making a smoothie allows for easier and better absorption of fibrous fruits and vegetables. As an additional bonus, smoothies provide one of the easiest and most convenient ways to exploit the powerful synergy between foods. In other words, pairing certain foods with others can enhance their innate nutritional value. There are several examples of these "dynamic duos" at play in this smoothie recipe including: yogurt and berries; wheat germ and spinach; and yogurt and spinach.

Here is how you make this meal…

Ingredients

½ cup frozen berries of choice (mixed, blueberries, strawberries or blackberries)

1 banana

1 packed handful of baby spinach

1 small container (about ¾ cups) of low-fat plain or vanilla Greek-style yogurt

1 tbsp toasted wheat germ

A splash of any 100% juice (I like pomegranate—lots of antioxidants) to allow for easy blending

3 tbsp ground hemp powder or protein powder of choice (optional)

Directions

Place all ingredients in a blender and blend until smooth.

Dr. Ann's NOTES

➤ There are countless ways to customize this smoothie recipe. In fact, the only thing that is a must is the frozen berries (frozen berries make the texture right and are too healthy for you to skip). You can add any additional fruit that you desire. I also love apples, grapes, kiwi, melon, peaches and plums in my smoothies. Although I would be happiest if you included some form of dark leafy greens, even sans greens this smoothie is wholesome and great for you.

➤ If you find that this smoothie doesn't keep your appetite at bay for three full hours, add one scoop of protein powder. I love ground hemp seed protein powder because it is a true "whole food"-based protein powder and one of the most nutritionally complete foods on the planet. But any variety of protein powder will do. Chia seeds or ground flax seeds are an excellent substitute for the wheat germ.

➤ Please note that I specifically ask you to use low-fat versus non-fat yogurt. Remember, fat-soluble nutrients require the presence of some fat to be absorbed efficiently.

➤ If you do not already own a Magic Bullet® blender, I highly recommend one. It Is affordable and fantastic for making individual smoothies.

Smoothie Basics: The Nutritional Benefits Of Mixing Fruit And "Greek-Style" Yogurt

Superstar Foods:
GREEK-STYLE YOGURT

Low-fat or non-fat, plain Greek-style yogurt is an exceptional food when it comes to nutrition and health. This yummy yogurt is strained to remove its liquid component, giving it a decadent and creamy texture that doubles its protein and lowers its sugar (lactose) content. A standard 5.3 ounce container of Greek-style yogurt has minimal to no fat, 15 grams of protein, and only 100 calories. For those who prefer yogurt a bit sweetened, Oikos® brand comes in a vanilla flavor that has just a teaspoon of added sugar versus the 3 or more teaspoons typically found in other flavored yogurts.

Kitchen Tips

> Be sure to wash fresh fruit thoroughly to reduce exposure to pesticides and harmful bacteria. It is best to perform what we call a "water bath." Let the produce sit in a sink of tepid water for 30 seconds, then swish it around for 30 more seconds. Drain the sink and rinse the produce thoroughly under running water.

> Remember that you can find both fresh and *frozen*, ready-to-eat fruit at most grocery stores. Keep bags of frozen berries in your freezer. Wholesale grocers like Costco® and Sam's® sell large bags with a convenient zippered opening for a great price.

> Always have one serving of fruit at breakfast and another for a snack.

> Berry-based fruit smoothies with soy milk, skim milk, plain yogurt or protein powder are delicious and nutritious. Add a hard-boiled omega-3 egg, wheat germ, or flaxseed to enhance it with some healthy omega-3 fats and other beneficial nutrients.

> Make fruit a first choice for dessert.

Beyond Fruit And Yogurt: Essential Foods To Always Have On Hand

10 Foods That You Will Always Find
IN DR. ANN'S FRIDGE

1. Large container of non-fat or low-fat plain Greek yogurt
2. Organic soy milk
3. Hummus
4. Free range eggs (from my nephew Boo who has a small chicken operation in his backyard) or store bought omega-3 eggs
5. At least four varieties of fresh fruit
6. At least six varieties of fresh vegetables
7. Organic half & half (yes, I put it in my one morning mug of coffee)
8. Grey Poupon® Harvest Course Ground Mustard®
9. Fresh salsa
10. Dinner leftovers

15 Foods That You Will Always Find
IN DR. ANN'S PANTRY

1. Almond butter
2. Organic quinoa
3. A variety of canned and dried beans
4. Canned red sockeye salmon
5. A variety of bagged teas
6. Steel cut oats or old-fashioned oats
7. Cocoa powder
8. Brown rice
9. Honey or molasses
10. Organic chicken broth
11. Food Should Taste Good® multigrain tortilla chips
12. Extra virgin olive oil
13. A variety of vinegars
14. Stone-ground grits
15. Dark chocolate bars

[WHAT'S RIGHT FOR BREAKFAST]
Healthy Cereal Topped With Fruit

NUMBER OF SERVINGS
1
NUMBER OF SERVINGS

www.welcoa.org ★ ©2013 Wellness Council of America

Cold cereals are the easiest and quickest way I know to get in a serving or more of whole grains and are a proven means to start your day on a healthy note. Studies show that people who include whole grain cereals in their breakfasts consume more essential nutrients, have an easier time managing their weight and are less likely to develop heart disease and type 2 diabetes. You can take your morning bowl of cereal from good to stellar by sprucing it up with the tasty and nutritious additions detailed below.

Here is how you make this meal…

Ingredients

1 serving (a single serving is generally ¾ to 1 ¼ cup—check the label) of any of the following cereals:

- ➤ Post® Grape Nuts®
- ➤ Post® Great Grains®
- ➤ Kellogg's® Wheat Chex®
- ➤ Kellogg's® Bran Flakes®
- ➤ Kellogg's® Frosted Mini-Wheats®
- ➤ Kashi® Heart-to-Heart®
- ➤ Kashi® Autumn Wheat®
- ➤ Kashi® Go Lean Crisp®
- ➤ Quaker® Oat Squares®
- ➤ Quaker® Oat Bran®

½ cup or more diced fruit of choice or berries (frozen or fresh)

1 tbsp toasted wheat germ or ground flax seeds

1 oz (1 small handful) nuts of choice, chopped

Skim or 1% milk or plain soy milk as desired

Directions

Pour dry cereal into a mug or bowl. Top with the remaining ingredients and dig in.

Dr. Ann's NOTES

- ➤ Of course, the star player in this healthy breakfast line-up is the right cereal. Like the examples I've listed in the ingredients, be sure to select a cereal that provides at least five grams of fiber and no more than 10 grams of sugar per serving. See the nutrition facts area on the cereal box for this info.

- ➤ If the added fruit doesn't provide enough sweetness for your taste buds, you can try adding one teaspoon of sugar, honey, maple syrup or molasses.

- ➤ Most grocery stores stock wheat germ in the cereal aisle. Kretschmer® is a common brand and it comes in a large glass jar. It has a delicious nutty taste and I can't say enough about the wonderful nutrients it provides.

- ➤ Buying your nuts and berries (frozen) in bulk will be much gentler on your pocketbook. Wholesale grocers carry large bags of each in several varieties. At any given moment, I always have at least two large bags of frozen berries in my freezer. Store your large containers of bulk nuts in your freezer.

- ➤ For a heftier dose of appetite-suppressive protein, feel free to substitute low-fat or non-fat Greek-style plain yogurt for the milk in your bowl of cereal. I do this because it is easier to eat on the run or commute without spilling on my lap!

©2013 Wellness Council of America®

Boost Your Fiber At Breakfast, Boost Your Will Power All Day

Superstar Foods:
WHEAT GERM

Get into the habit of sprinkling a couple of tablespoons of toasted wheat germ in your morning cereal. This three-second endeavor provides a huge boost in folic acid and Vitamin E (wheat germ provides more than any other food) along with a nice dose of fiber, magnesium, zinc, and omega-3 fats. Incidentally, these specific nutrients are the same ones Americans are most likely to be deficient in.

Dr. Ann Recommends
SMALLER IS BETTER

When choosing your produce, always opt for the smallest varieties. The smaller the fruit or vegetable, the higher its skin to flesh ratio. Their goodness (especially the phytochemicals and fiber) concentrates in their skin and just beneath. Examples: grape tomatoes over beefsteak tomatoes, wild blueberries over conventional, fingerling potatoes over russets, miniature eggplant over larger, etc.

Boosting Your
WILL POWER

Given our toxic food culture, cultivating self-discipline on the eating front is an invaluable practice. According to an intriguing recent study, keeping some high-risk, tempting foods in your midst is an effective means to build will power. Investigators found that study subjects who had been previously tempted by forbidden foods exercised more self-restraint when offered these foods compared to those not previously exposed.

Use Your Extras: Breakfast, Lunch & Dinner

Dr. Ann Recommends

UPGRADE YOUR MEAL

Here are 10 simple ways to boost the nutrition of your favorite meals with great-tasting extras in less than 10 seconds.

1. **Add 1-2 tablespoons of toasted wheat germ to your morning cereal, yogurt or smoothies.** Wheat germ has a slightly sweet, yet nutty flavor and is loaded with minerals, vitamin E, fiber, protein, omega-3 fats and almost one-third of an adult's daily requirement for folate. You can find it in your grocer's cereal aisle.

2. **Sprinkle cinnamon on your morning cereal, yogurt, bagels or toast.** This tasty spice provides remarkable health benefits through its ability to enhance the action of the hormone, insulin. Increased insulin activity translates to improved glucose and cholesterol metabolism, and protection from type 2 diabetes and cardiovascular disease.

3. **Add brocco sprouts to your salads and sandwiches.** Developed by cancer researchers from John Hopkins, these sprouts are filled with fiber and vitamin C, and are unique because of their anti-cancer prowess. These tasty sprouts contain 20-100 times more of the natural cancer-prevention agent, sulforaphane, than mature broccoli.

4. **Add sun-dried tomatoes to your pizza, pasta and sandwiches.** Low in calories, but high in flavor, they provide all of the spectacular goodness in tomatoes (fiber, B vitamins, potassium, vitamin C, lycopene) in a super-concentrated form. Lycopene is now world famous for prostate cancer protection.

5. **Add fresh salsa to your egg, veggie, pasta or poultry dishes** for a boost in lycopene, vitamin C, potassium and fiber. Most grocery stores now carry ready made cartons of fresh salsa in the refrigerator sections.

6. **Spice up your bean, poultry and rice dishes with turmeric or curry spices.** Both are teeming with the golden yellow pigment, curcumin, which is now world-famous for its anti-inflammatory power. Inflammation plays a fundamental role in the formation of many chronic diseases including cardiovascular disease, obesity, cancer and Alzheimer's.

7. **Go nuts!** Throw a small handful (about 1 ounce) of nuts (any that suit your palate) into salads, soups, sauces or other prepared dishes. These delectable morsels of good health score a perfect 10 when it comes to a heart-healthy performance. Of nuts' eight nutritional attributes, seven provide specific cardiovascular benefits. It's no surprise that several studies report that eating an ounce of nuts five days a week can reduce your risk of death from heart disease by a whopping 30-55 percent!

8. **Add canned pumpkin to your soups, pancakes, muffins and other baked goods** This convenient and inexpensive item is one of the most nutrient-packed foods available. Low in calories, high in fiber and providing the most concentrated package of disease-fighting carotenoids known, canned pumpkin is an under-utilized superstar food. Carotenoids play a central role in the health of your heart, eyes, skin and immune system.

9. **Add pesto to your sandwiches, sauces and pastas.** Pesto is decadently delicious and provide nothing but 100 percent pure heart-healthy ingredients—fresh basil, pine nuts, garlic and olive oil.

10. **Throw some berries (frozen are just as healthy as fresh) into your pancake mix, smoothies, yogurt or cereals.** Berries are my top-rated fruit—loaded with fiber, vitamin C, folic acid and super-potent antioxidants.

[WHAT'S RIGHT FOR BREAKFAST]
Breakfast Burrito

This burrito puts a fresh new twist on the best of breakfast. You get your whole grains, protein and produce in a single warm and delicious package. Between the eggs, cheese, and beans, this protein-packed breakfast should easily satisfy you until lunch time.

Here is how you make this meal…

Ingredients

2 large omega-3 eggs

1, 6–8 inch 100% whole wheat tortilla

¼ cup shredded part-skim mozzarella or 2% milk cheddar cheese

2 tbsp or more of salsa (I prefer Garden Fresh Gourmet®)

2–3 tbsp rinsed canned black beans or hummus (optional)

Directions

Scramble the eggs to your liking in a small skillet sprayed with pan spray. Layer eggs across the center portion of the tortilla. Top the eggs with the remaining ingredients. Fold in the sides of the tortilla and roll it up to create a spill-free package.

Dr. Ann's NOTES

➤ Please be sure to get 100% whole wheat or 100% whole grain tortillas. Otherwise, you will be missing out on the benefits of whole grains. Many brands are available.

➤ I encourage you to add in the beans (any variety will work) or hummus because it is a tasty way to amp up B-vitamins, protein and fiber.

➤ For more of a spicy kick, shake a little garlic powder, cumin or oregano over the eggs.

➤ If you are feeling extra motivated, throw in a few slices of fresh avocado or a heaping tablespoon of guacamole.

➤ If you are in a hurry, wrap the burrito up tightly in some foil and take it with you.

➤ Any piece of fresh fruit is a great accompaniment to this dish.

Proteinize And Fiberize Your Breakfast Burrito With Black Beans

Superstar Foods:
BLACK BEANS

Cheap, convenient and oh-so-tasty, black beans are the cream of the bean crop. These black beauties have megawatt nutritional goodness including a hefty dose of fiber and protein, a full spectrum of minerals, loads of B-vitamins, and antioxidant power that rivals red grapes and cranberries. Enjoy them canned, fresh, frozen, or dried.

Love Vegetables In Your Breakfast Burrito? Roast 'em!

Kitchen Tip:
ROAST YOUR VEGGIES

Roasting is one of the easiest and tastiest ways to prepare your veggies. It preserves their nutrients and concentrates their natural sugars and flavors, which makes them particularly yummy to even the pickiest palates. Roasting also dramatically shrinks a vegetable's size (because it removes their water), making it easier to consume more in one sitting. Based on my culinary experience, cauliflower, broccoli, sweet potatoes, carrots, Brussel sprouts, asparagus, onions, and bell peppers best lend themselves to roasting. Simply place your vegetables on a baking sheet or casserole dish, drizzle or mist with extra-virgin olive oil, sprinkle with kosher salt, and roast at 375-400 degrees until lightly browned (about 15-20 minutes).

Maximize Your Breakfast Burrito With The Power Of Omega-3 Eggs

Superstar Foods:
OMEGA-3 EGGS

Eggs are healthiest if boiled or poached; however, they are still great for you when prepared other ways. Keep a carton of hard boiled eggs in the refrigerator at all times for a great, grab-and-go protein source.

In Praise Of
OMEGA-3 EGGS

Eggs have always been a cheap, delicious and convenient source of high quality, low-fat protein that comes along with B vitamins, vitamin E and iron. Thanks to modern food technology, some eggs are now healthier than ever. Many egg producers now fortify their chicken feed with omega-3 fats (usually from fish meal) which means that this superstar fat gets incorporated into the egg yolk. These "omega-3 eggs" are available at all grocery outlets. You will pay a bit more, but it's well worth it as these eggs are second only to seafood as the most plentiful food source of the long-chained omega-3 fats like DHA. Simply look for "DHA" or "omega-3" on the label. Eggland's Best® (white carton) are a popular brand and have also been voted America's "best-tasting" egg by the American Culinary Institute.

[WHAT'S RIGHT FOR BREAKFAST]

Peanut Butter and Banana Roll-Up

NUMBER OF SERVINGS · NUMBER OF SERVINGS
1

Peanut butter along with any other nut butters (like almond butter) pack an amazing nutritional punch and are a great way to incorporate vegetable-based protein at breakfast. Nut butters are exploding with heart-healthy nutrients including monounsaturated fats, vitamin E, B vitamins, minerals, and potent antioxidants. In fact, studies repeatedly find that people who regularly include nuts (including peanut butter!) in their diets are up to 40 percent less likely to die of cardiovascular disease than those who don't include them. And it is a myth that nuts and peanut butter are uniquely fattening. In fact, studies show that people who regularly include nuts (including peanut butter) in their diets are *leaner* and gain less weight over time than those who don't. Of course limits are in order—enjoy your peanut butter or almond butter, but stick to no more than two tablespoons a day.

Here is how you make this meal…

Ingredients

1, 6–8 inch 100% whole wheat tortilla

1 ½ tbsp peanut butter or almond butter

1 small banana or ½ large banana sliced lengthwise

1 tbsp wheat germ or ground flax seed

Directions

Spread the peanut butter or almond butter across the center of the tortilla. Layer the banana slices on top of the nut butter. Sprinkle with the wheat germ or ground flax and roll up the tortilla or fold it like you would a burrito.

Dr. Ann's NOTES

> Although I think peanut butter (and almond butter) and bananas are delectable together, you can substitute the banana with any fruit you like.

> Apple or pear slices taste great with peanut butter and add a refreshing crunch. If you can't put your hand on any fresh fruit, a convenient back up would be a berry-based fruit spread (not jelly or jam).

> Berry-based fruit spreads serve as a healthy substitute if you don't have any fresh fruit on hand. These spreads are loaded with potent antioxidants and generally have less sugar and more fiber than standard jellies and jams. I am particularly fond of the Polaner® All Fruit With Fiber® brand.

> If you have never tried almond butter give it whirl because it is heavenly.

> A cold glass of skim milk or soy milk is the perfect beverage to pair with this breakfast and will keep the peanut butter from sticking to your throat.

> During the winter, a mug of hot cocoa (made from real cocoa powder) is another delicious pairing.

Get Milk! The Best Beverage To Partner With A Peanut Butter & Banana Roll-Up

Dr. Ann Recommends
SOY MILK

If you're lactose intolerant or are seeking a more plant-based diet, organic plain calcium-fortified soy milk is an excellent replacement for cow's milk. Soy milk provides complete protein, omega-3 fats and an abundance of key vitamins and minerals along with health-protective plant chemicals called isoflavones. I love it by the glass and most anyone will enjoy it with their cereal or blended into a smoothie. Other cow's milk alternatives like almond milk or rice milk are nutritional weaklings compared to plain soy milk.

Peanut Butter & Bananas Make Dr. Ann's Top Ten List of Convenience Foods!

Dr. Ann's Top Ten
CONVENIENCE FOODS

1. Prepared tabbouleh (NeJame's® or Hannah® brands)
2. Washed, bagged organic baby spinach
3. Fresh salsa (Jack's® or Garden Fresh Gourmet®)
4. Canned beans
5. Frozen berries (large bag Pacific Meadow® wild organic blueberries—available from wholesale grocers like Costco®)
6. Toasted wheat germ (Kretschmer®)
7. Organic baby carrots
8. Canned wild Alaskan salmon (red sockeye)
9. Hummus
10. Uncle Ben's® Ready Whole Grain Rice® (90 seconds in the microwave and its done!)

Let's Make A List!

Dr. Ann's Recommends
HEALTHY GROCERY SHOPPING

Achieving nutritional excellence begins with making the right choices in the grocery store. In fact, much of the work of healthy eating is done right in your grocery aisles. The following "rules of the road" will guide you through your travels in the grocery store to ensure a successful and nutritious trip. Keep these ground rules in mind as you make your way from one area to another. Be sure to concentrate on the periphery of the grocery store. The outside aisles hold the life-preserving foods nature provides. Many interior aisles contain an endless array of factory-made, nutritionally defunct processed foods—so travel quickly through them or avoid them all together.

Here are the "rules of the road" for the basic destinations within the grocery store:

Produce. Go for variety, deep rich color, and more, more, more! All forms of produce have something beneficial to offer, but some are especially healthy. These superstars include: broccoli, cabbage, cauliflower, Brussels sprouts, kale, collards, carrots, garlic, onions, leeks, sweet potatoes, dark leafy greens, tomatoes, winter squash, asparagus, red/orange/yellow bell peppers, berries, cherries, plums, any whole citrus, cantaloupe, kiwi, mango, peaches, pears, red grapes, apples, and dried or fresh apricots. Avoid white potatoes, especially if you're overweight or diabetic.

Dairy. Select reduced fat, low fat, or skim. Avoid whole milk and full fat cheeses. Choose trans fat-free margarine spreads instead of butter or stick margarine. Plain soy milk is a great alternative to cow's milk.

Meat/Seafood. Concentrate your efforts on seafood and poultry. Try to limit red meat and processed meats like bacon and sausage. Choose lean cuts of beef and pork if or when you do purchase these items.

Eggs. Choose the omega-3-fortified varieties. Look for omega-3 or DHA on the label.

Frozen Foods. Frozen fruits, vegetables, seafood, and poultry are just as nutritious as fresh. Avoid frozen vegetables with added butter or sauces. Avoid frozen fruits with added sugar.

Grain Products/Starches. Choose 100% whole grain products. Look for "100% whole grain or 100% whole wheat" on the label. Physically intact whole grains like brown rice, barley, oats, quinoa, etc. have a health edge over 100% whole grain breads. Choose whole wheat or multigrain brands of pasta, like Barilla Plus®.

Canned Goods. Canned foods are generally inferior to fresh, but the following retain their nutritional value: any form of tomato products, beans, and 100% pumpkin. Choose reduced sodium varieties when available. Canned salmon, chunk-lite tuna, sardines, and oysters are convenient and healthy proteins.

Beverages. Coffee, loose leaf or bagged teas, herbal teas, V8® or 100% vegetable/tomato juice and water are your best choices. If weight is not an issue, you can consume 100% fruit juice in moderation.

Condiments. Hummus, bean dips, salsa, tabbouleh, bruschetta, horseradish, guacamole, pesto, and sun-dried tomatoes, are healthy choices. Vinegar, ketchup, mayonnaise (olive oil or canola-based mayonnaises are best), hot sauce, mustards, tahini, and light soy sauce are acceptable choices. All herbs and spices—dried or fresh—are fantastic. Select olive oil or canola oil-based vinaigrettes for your salad dressings. Avoid fat-free (too much sugar) and creamy varieties.

Cooking Oil. Your best choices are extra virgin olive oil and canola oil. Nut-based oils (walnut, sesame, etc) are also healthy choices if called for in recipes. Grapeseed oil and sesame oil are great for stir fry's or high heat. Pan sprays are wonderful.

Cereals. To make a healthy selection, check the label for five grams or more of fiber and 10 grams or less of sugar per serving.

[WHAT'S RIGHT FOR BREAKFAST]

Dr. Ann's Homemade Granola

NUMBER OF SERVINGS • NUMBER OF SERVINGS
12

Homemade granola is so easy to make and when it comes to taste, value, and healthfulness this recipe puts the store bought varieties to shame. We always have a big batch of this granola on hand at my house. I enjoy it so much that I include a small handful after most of my dinners because it gives me that tiny bit of sweetness I crave. I don't fight my cravings, but I do address them with a prudent portion of something wholesome and nutritious.

Here is how you make this meal…

Ingredients

5 cups of old-fashioned oats

1 ½ cups nuts of choice, chopped coarsely

1 cup shredded coconut (optional)

1 ½ cups dried fruit of choice (raisins, apricots, cranberries, etc)

½ cup molasses

1 tsp vanilla extract

3 tsp cinnamon

¼ cup canola oil

Directions

Preheat the oven to 325 degrees. Place the dry ingredients in a large mixing bowl and stir until thoroughly combined. Add the molasses, oil, and vanilla and stir until the dry ingredients are evenly coated. Spread the mixture evenly on a baking sheet with sides and bake at 325 degrees until light brown and toasted (about 25–30 minutes). For even cooking, carefully stir the granola mixture every 10 minutes. Remove the granola from the oven and allow it to cool— it will become crunchier as it cools down. Store the granola in an airtight container at room temperature or in the freezer in a Ziploc® bag. Makes about eight cups. One serving is ⅔ of a cup.

Dr. Ann's

> I encourage you to get creative and inventive with this recipe. Experiment with various nuts and seeds. My standard nut/seed combo is walnuts, pine nuts, sunflower seeds, and pecans.

> You can change things up with the dried fruit too. I prefer apricots, peaches, raisins, and plums because I know they have the least sugar.

> I always sweeten my granola with molasses because I love its rich, complex flavor. Molasses is also rich in key minerals like iron and potassium. As an alternative, you can use honey or maple syrup.

> I love to use this granola to make a quick breakfast parfait. In a large glass or plastic cup, alternate layers of the granola with Greek-style plain or vanilla yogurt and fresh or frozen berries.

> If your family enjoys this granola as much as mine does, I recommend that you double the recipe each time you make it. This will save you time.

Spice Up Your Granola With Cinnamon And Walnuts

Superstar Foods:
CINNAMON

Cinnamon, like many other spices, is emerging as a true wonder food. It contains potent plant compounds that improve the metabolism of blood sugar and cholesterol and may also be helpful for appetite control. One recent study found that cinnamon helps slow down the rate of gastric (stomach) emptying, which can help you feel fuller longer. I keep an extra large container of ground cinnamon handy in my cupboard and sprinkle it liberally in my cereal, yogurt, coffee and fruit-based desserts.

Superstar Foods:
WALNUTS

Walnuts score a perfect 10 when it comes to protecting the cardiovascular system. Moreover, walnuts are a big winner on other numerous fronts. In the past few years, studies have shown that walnuts likely provide protection against breast cancer, prostate cancer, dementia, macular degeneration and even stress. As nuts go, walnuts are the richest source of superstar omega-3 fats and can boast the highest overall antioxidant power. I buy walnuts raw in bulk and throw them into my salads, oatmeal, grain dishes, and of course, right in my mouth for a snack.

Dr. Ann's Answers To Your Hunger

Reining In
YOUR APPETITE

➤ **Feel full with fruits and veggies.** They are high in fiber and water, while low in calories. The fiber volume in fruits and veggies has a powerful appetite suppressive effect. The name of the game is regularly "bulking up" meals and snacks with as many hefty, yet low-calorie, fruits and veggies as possible.

➤ **Eat slowly.** It takes at least 20 minutes for the satiety signals released from your stomach to reach and quiet the appetite centers in your brain.

➤ **Eat mindfully.** Be constantly aware when you are eating. Mindless eating, especially in front of distracting influences like television, increases caloric intake. Always sit down at a table to eat.

➤ **Plate anything (meals, snacks, dessert etc.) you eat.** You know exactly how much you're eating if you see it on a plate. If you eat directly out of the box or container, it's very easy to lose track and/or over eat.

➤ **Buy small packages/containers of high risk, high calorie foods.** The bigger the package size, the more we tend to serve ourselves.

➤ **Downsize your dinner-ware.** We tend to eat less when we use smaller plates, bowls and utensils.

➤ **Keep meals and snacks "flavor-simple."** The greater the flavor variety, the more we eat. Whole, fresh, unprocessed foods have the most simplified flavor profile and are typically the very best choices.

➤ **Minimize visits to buffets.** The greater the variety or selection of food choices, the more we tend to eat. Unless you're loading up at the salad bar with fruits and veggies, you should try to avoid buffets.

[WHAT'S RIGHT FOR BREAKFAST]

Smoked Salmon (Lox) and Avocado Bagel Sandwich

NUMBER OF SERVINGS
1

Sometimes we just need a change of taste and this bagel sandwich will break anyone out of the breakfast doldrums. It capitalizes on the scrumptious combination of salmon, capers, and red onions. Better yet, it promises to please your heart and brain as much as it does your taste buds. The salmon is loaded with superstar omega-3 fats and both capers and red onions offer some of the highest concentration of antioxidant flavonoids in the entire plant food kingdom. The whole grain bagel or English muffin rounds out this breakfast sandwich with a nice dose of healthy carbs and counts as up to two servings of your recommended daily three servings of whole grains.

Here is how you make this meal…

Ingredients

1 100% whole wheat bagel (3.5 oz or less) or 100% whole wheat English muffin, toasted

3 slices of avocado (about ¼ of an avocado)

2 slices of smoked salmon (2–3 oz)

2 very thin slices of red onion

1 tsp of capers

2 tbsp plain low-fat or non-fat Greek-style yogurt

½ tsp chopped fresh dill (optional)

Directions

Spread the yogurt on one half of the toasted bagel. Top it with (in this order) the capers, onions, salmon, avocado and dill (if using). Cover with the other half of the toasted bagel/English muffin to complete your sandwich.

Dr. Ann's NOTES

➤ Although it won't have that huge hit of omega-3 fats, you can substitute deli turkey or chicken for the smoked salmon. Or try a poached egg.

➤ You can use a squirt or two of horseradish sauce (I love the Boar's Head® brand) in place of the yogurt. This substitution adds a spicy kick that complements the sub-dued flavors in the avo-cado.

➤ You can wrap this bagel sandwich in foil and eat it during your morning com-mute.

Avocado & Salmon: Keys To The Perfect, Atypical Breakfast Sandwich

Superstar Foods:
AVOCADOS

I am always amazed by the number of people who consider avocados unhealthy or fattening. The delicious reality is that they are true wonder foods. Avocados are filled with heart-healthy monounsaturated fats that lower bad (LDL) cholesterol while boosting good (HDL) cholesterol. They are also packed with fiber, vitamin E, B vitamins and special cholesterol-lowering plant substances called phytosterols. Avocados have even made it on the list of the top 20 most potent antioxidant foods. This unique package of nutritional attributes renders avocados oh-so-valuable for heart and brain health— so go guacamole!

Farm-Raised vs
WILD SALMON

About 70% of the fresh salmon consumed in this country is farm-raised. Although I consider farm-raised (also know as Atlantic salmon) to be an important source of valuable omega-3 fats and healthy protein for many Americans, it is inferior in nutritional quality to wild Alaskan salmon. Both have equivalent amounts of omega-3 fats, but farm-raised salmon has more unhealthy saturated fat, a much higher omega-6: omega-3 ratio and may contain traces of antibiotics and environmental contaminants like PCB's. Fresh wild Alaskan salmon is generally available a few months out of the year, but can always be found canned and frequently frozen. Wild salmon is always my first choice.

©2013 Wellness Council of America

This Is Only The Beginning. The Options Are Endless!

Dr. Ann Recommends
DON'T SKIP BREAKFAST!

Because life is real and mornings can be hectic, here are some grab-and-go breakfast options for you. Remember, even a piece of fresh fruit is better than nothing at all!

➤ 1 ½ ounces (healthy handful) of mixed nuts or your nut of choice. Throw them in a Ziploc® bag and grab a piece of fresh fruit.

➤ Two part-skim mozzarella cheese sticks with a piece of fresh fruit.

➤ One individual container of Greek-style yogurt with a piece of fresh fruit.

➤ Two hard boiled omega-3 eggs with a piece of fresh fruit.

➤ Two granola bars (I prefer Kashi®) topped with a thin layer of peanut or almond butter (place together like a sandwich to keep your fingers free of the nut butter) with a piece of fresh fruit.

➤ One cup of finger friendly healthy dry cereal (I like Quaker® Oat Squares® or Kashi® Cinnamon Harvest®) with a piece of fresh fruit.

➤ 1 ½ ounces of roasted soy nuts with a piece of fresh fruit.

➤ Two squares of dark chocolate with a banana (my favorite).

Breakfast Of CHAMPS

Boost Your Brain Power With Breakfast

After an overnight fast, your brain's only source of fuel—namely glucose—is at an all-time low. Skipping breakfast is a major brain drain because it deprives brain cells of their much needed energy source. Eating the right breakfast provides your brain with an immediate source of high quality fuel along with the key nutrients it requires for optimal function.

Breakfast For Weight Control

Eating breakfast enhances weight control through many mechanisms including: boosting metabolism, boosting energy (thus calorie-burning), diminishing hunger over the course of the day and reducing insulin levels (elevated insulin levels are associated with a sluggish metabolism).

Breakfast Beverages,
Done Right

encourage you to pair your breakfast with the right beverage. The healthiest choices are:

➤ **Water.** Remember that tap water is infinitely cheaper and more regulated than bottled. Do not waste your money on vitamin or fitness waters!

➤ **1% or skim milk.** I prefer you drink organic varieties.

➤ **Plain organic soy milk.** Avoid the flavored versions because they have too much added sugar.

➤ **100% vegetable or tomato juice.** Choose reduced-sodium varieties.

➤ **Freshly brewed, unsweetened tea.** Choose loose leaf or bagged; not powdered or bottled. Add a twist of lemon or lime to enhance its flavor and antioxidant capacity. Herbal teas are fine, too.

➤ **Coffee.** Black and unsweetened is best. If you prefer cream, low-fat or skim milk or powdered non-fat dry milk is healthier than half-and-half.

➤ **A small glass (4 ounces) of any 100% fruit juice.** 100% fruit juices that are cloudy with sediment on the bottom are best. If you are overweight, inactive, diabetic, or prediabetic you should avoid fruit juices.

Dr. Ann Recommends
DRINK YOUR WATER!

According to Vanderbilt University scientists, having a drink of ordinary water (no designer "vitamin" waters needed!) can make you feel more alert and even kick up your metabolism a bit. Apparently, drinking water stimulates our sympathetic nervous system. The lead researcher calculated that drinking three additional 16-ounce glasses of water a day could translate to as much as five pounds of weight loss in a year! I am going to go drink some now!

Enjoy
GREEN TEA

Get into the habit of drinking freshly brewed green tea daily. This superstar elixir of good health provides one of the easiest and quickest ways to infuse your body and your brain with antioxidants. Antioxidants are special chemicals that provide protection against cancer, heart disease, cataracts, arthritis, skin wrinkling, and even the aging process itself. Brewed tea has more antioxidant power than any other fruit or vegetable. And consider this—where can you find a food that can decrease your cardiovascular risk, boost your immunity, likely decrease your cancer risk and kick up your metabolism all for zero calories? I sip on green tea throughout the day.

1. All forms of freshly brewed tea (green, black, white, and oolong) are teeming with antioxidants, but green tea is uniquely high in a chemical called EGCG. EGCG is one of the most potent antioxidants ever discovered and is being investigated vigorously for its cancer-protective properties.

2. Please note that many of tea's antioxidants are destroyed during processing so powdered, bottled, and decaffeinated teas are not recommended.

3. For best results, steep your green tea (bagged or loose leaf) for at least three minutes and squeeze the bag at the end of steeping to take full advantage of its antioxidant punch.

4. Avoid adding milk or cream as studies have shown that they hinder beneficial tea chemicals.

5. Do add a twist of lemon or lime to your tea. Its vitamin C dramatically boosts the absorption of the tea's antioxidants.

6. If you must, sweeten with *a little* honey, sugar, or stevia.

Eat **Right** For Lunch

P acking a healthy lunch is one of the surest ways to trim your budget and your waistline. And with the ideas that follow, your lunch experience can be as delicious and easy as it is nutritious.

Just like a healthy breakfast, this mid-day feeding should include some lean protein along with a nice dose of "slow-release" carbs (fruits, non-starchy vegetables, beans and/or whole grains) to keep your brain and body fueled through the afternoon. And don't forget to round things off with some healthy fat. After all, fat makes our food taste good and the right fats—as featured in these lunch recipes—truly guard and improve your health!

[WHAT'S RIGHT FOR LUNCH]

Entrée Salad de Jour

NUMBER OF SERVINGS · NUMBER OF SERVINGS
1

Dr. Ann's
NOTES

Salads offer an unprecedented opportunity to dazzle your taste buds while tapping into the remarkable health-boosting power plant foods can provide. Entrée salads, prepared as follows, are my number one rated lunch for those who want to revitalize their health, operate at the top of their game, and reduce their carbon foot print! A big salad made right is also my top lunch pick for those who want to shed some weight. About 12 years ago while still in my family medicine practice, I decided to make the switch from the hospital cafeteria's hot food bar to their comprehensive salad bar. It was astounding how much more energized, alert and GOOD I felt through the remainder of the afternoon. Even my nurses noticed the additional spring in my step and I have been happily hooked ever since. I feel sure that once you experience the all-over goodness and healing power salads so generously provide, you will do exactly as I do and never let a day go by without eating a big, fresh, colorful salad.

Here is how you make this meal…

Ingredients

2 cups dark leafy greens of choice (spinach, romaine, mixed mesclun, red leaf, etc.)

3 or more ⅓ to ½ cup servings of vegetables and/or fruit of choice. Go for the superstars—red onion, carrots, broccoli or cauliflower florets, tomatoes, bell peppers, olives, berries, avocados, apples, cantaloupe, and red grapes.

1 tbsp nuts or seeds of choice

3 ounces (the size of a deck of cards) lean protein—skinless turkey or chicken, hard-cooked eggs, low-fat cottage cheese, shrimp, tuna, tofu, tempeh or beans.

2 tbsp vinaigrette (See my homemade dressing recipes on the following page).

Directions

Combine all ingredients in a large bowl and toss thoroughly with the vinaigrette. Eat every last bite and feel the health.

> ➤ If you don't have time to prepare your lunch salad from home, most casual dining restaurants and delis have fully loaded salad bars as a convenient back-up.

> ➤ Whether you make your own from home or a nearby restaurant, always throw in as many brightly colored fruits and veggies as possible. Seeing color and variety in foods stimulates appetite (which is why they make M&Ms® multi-colored!).

> ➤ The bulk and fiber in your salad goes a long way towards filling up your stomach, but for optimal appetite control the lean protein is a must.

> ➤ Do not sabotage the nutritional excellence of your salad by adding the white stuff—pasta salad, potato salad, and croutons.

> ➤ The healthiest dressings are an olive oil-based vinaigrette or plain olive oil and vinegar. A reduced fat variety is acceptable. Definitely avoid the full-fat thicker varieties like ranch and blue cheese as the excess calories can really mount. Avoid fat-free dressings too because they are high in added sugar and you need some fat to absorb the stellar array of antioxidant carontenoids housed in those awesome veggies.

Get Into The Habit Of Making Your Own Salad Dressings

Mixing your own salad dressings is quick—about five minutes to prepare—and they are tastier, healthier and more economical than store brands. Here are three delicious options you can make:

Make Your Own... BALSAMIC VINAIGRETTE

- ¼ cup extra virgin olive oil
- 2 tbsp balsamic vinegar or any vinegar of choice
- A pinch of sugar
- 2 cloves garlic, minced
- 1 tbsp Dijon mustard (I love Grey Poupon® Harvest Course Ground®)

Whisk ingredients in a cup or small bowl until well blended. Store in an airtight container in your refrigerator.

Make Your Own... HONEY-LIME DRESSING

- ¼ cup fresh lime juice
- 1 garlic clove, minced
- 2 tbsp honey
- ¼ cup extra virgin olive oil
- 2 ½ tbsp finely chopped fresh cilantro
- 1 tsp chopped jalapeño pepper (optional)

Whisk ingredients in a cup or small bowl until well blended. Store in an airtight container in your refrigerator.

Make Your Own... GINGER-ORANGE DRESSING

- ½ cup peanut or canola oil
- ¼ cup O.J. concentrate, thawed
- 2 tbsp seasoned rice vinegar
- 2 tbsp finely chopped ginger

Whisk ingredients in a cup or small bowl until well blended. Store in an airtight container in your refrigerator.

Get Into The Habit Of Other Great Flavors!
Condiments And FLAVOR ENHANCERS

- Use these condiments freely—mustard, salsa, pesto, hot sauce, light soy sauce, horseradish, and tahini.
- Lemons, limes, vinegar or vinegar-based sauces and dressings are excellent for lowering the glycemic index of carbohydrates. This is good for your metabolism and overall health.
- If a recipe calls for mayonnaise, use half mayonnaise and half plain Greek-style yogurt; no one will ever know the difference.

Extra Virgin Olive Oil: The Cornerstone Of Great Salad Dressings And Great Health

Getting The Most From
EXTRA VIRGIN OLIVE OIL

Why is it good for me?
Olive oil has a number of health benefits. It is filled with heart-healthy mono-unsaturated fats that can lower LDL (bad) cholesterol levels and boost HDL (good) cholesterol levels. It is also teeming with potent antioxidant and anti-inflammatory agents called polyphenols that provide broad spectrum health protection. It is not surprising that cultures that consume lots of olive oil have lower rates of cancer, Alzheimer's disease, arthritis and heart disease.

How should it be eaten?
For optimal health benefits, consume the "extra virgin" form of olive oil. Use it in foods prepared cold, at room temperature or with low to moderate heat. Olive oil is highly susceptible to oxidation when exposed to high temperatures and oxidized fats are unhealthy. "Extra virgin" implies that the oil has been extracted from the olives by a gentle pressing process versus heat or chemical extraction which can damage the healthy compounds in olives and oxidize its fats. Extra virgin olive oil has the highest concentration of valuable antioxidant polyphenols.

How often?
Daily. For optimal health, the majority of your fat calories should come from the monounsaturated class of fats. Olive oil is one of the four primary food sources of monounsaturated fats (the others are canola oil, nuts/seeds, and avocados).

Should we be concerned about the fat?
If consumed as part of a balanced, calorie-appropriate diet, absolutely not! Olive oil's monounsaturated fats and beneficial plant compounds quite literally improve and protect your health. When you drizzle that freshly baked whole grain bread with a little extra virgin olive oil (instead of slapping butter on it), you can definitely feel good about it.

PB & J

with a Side of Fresh Fruit

NUMBER OF SERVINGS • NUMBER OF SERVINGS •
1

When done right—this American classic makes for a simple, super-quick and very wholesome lunch. For me, a PB & J paired with a cold glass of milk is a definite comfort food and a lunch that I can always prepare no matter how past due my trip to the grocery store is. This iconic sandwich is underappreciated on the nutrition front and I am pleased to set the record straight. As prepared as follows, *this PB & J* provides two servings of whole grains, a delicious dose of healthy monounsaturated fat, vitamin E, B vitamins, several key minerals, and plant protein, along with a nice touch of vitamin C and powerful antioxidants. And believe it or not, peanut butter provides the compound resveratrol—yes, the same miracle compound (at least in the lab!) found in red wine that is famously touted for its anti-aging properties.

Here is how you make this meal…

Ingredients

2 tbsp smooth or crunchy peanut butter or nut butter of choice

1 ½ tbsp berry-based fruit spread (Polaner® or Smuckers® Simply Fruit® are good brands)

2 slices 100% whole wheat or 100% whole grain bread (look for 100% on the label)

Directions

Spread the peanut butter evenly over one slice of bread. Layer the fruit spread over the peanut butter and top with the other slice of bread.

Dr. Ann's NOTES

> ➤ To add some bulk, fiber and additional nutrients to this meal, I highly recommend that you pair it with a piece of fresh fruit. If you want to keep things "all in the sandwich," layer some sliced apples, pears or banana over the top of the peanut butter in lieu of the fruit spread.

> ➤ To dramatically ratchet up this sandwich's nutritional prowess, I highly recommend you sprinkle a tablespoon of wheat germ over the peanut butter (it only takes five seconds).

> ➤ Also, please note that the healthiest peanut butters are the "natural" brands (check labels).

> ➤ Any other nut butters (like almond butter) are great for you. My palate is borderline-addicted to almond butter.

PB & J: The Dynamic Duo Of The American Lunch Is A Protein Booster For Energy!

Stay Energetic And
FIGHT FATIGUE

1. **Be sure to have some high quality protein at each meal.**
   - ➤ The digestion of protein gives rise to a prolonged and sustained blood glucose level, which translates to a steady and robust energy level.
   - ➤ My top protein picks are omega-3 fortified eggs, beans, fish, skinless poultry, shellfish, nuts, seeds, whole soy foods and Greek-style plain yogurt.

2. **Indulge in an ounce or two of high quality dark chocolate.**
   - ➤ This delectable treat provides just the right amount of sugar and caffeine to jump-start dwindling energy levels and is loaded with some of the most powerful antioxidants yet documented. These antioxidant flavanols enhance blood flow which provides an additional energy boost.

3. **Drink a cup of freshly brewed green tea.** Tea provides a modest amount of energy boosting caffeine, along with potent antioxidants called catechins that increase blood flow. Unsweetened tea is the only food I know of that can boost energy, enhance immunity, likely prevent cancer, and protect against heart disease for zero calories!

4. **Eat more beans!** I consider beans one of nature's most perfect energy-boosting foods. They are a rich source of the body's preferred fuel—glucose—that's released slowly (this translates to more sustained energy). In addition, they are chock full of several B vitamins and minerals that play a key role in brain function and energy production.

Dr. Ann Recommends
OTHER DUOS

We now know that certain foods are synergistic with one another when it comes to boosting your health. Meaning, combining them will give you that much more nutritional bang for your efforts. Here are some tasty and healthy dynamic duos:

- ➤ Tomatoes and olive oil
- ➤ Garlic and fish
- ➤ Tea and lemon (or any other citrus)
- ➤ Tomatoes and broccoli
- ➤ Turmeric and black pepper
- ➤ Apples or blueberries and yogurt

PB & J Is Just The Start Of How You Can Lose Weight And Save On Food Costs

Tips For Trimming Your
WAISTLINE & BUDGET

1. **Control your portions!** This can certainly trim your grocery bill and restaurant bill. Recent scientific evidence finds that consistently controlling portions may be the fastest route to weight loss. According to one published study, controlling portions increased the chances of successful weight loss almost four fold!

2. **Dump sugary beverages**—sodas, fruit juices/drinks, sport drinks, etc. These liquid sugars cost money, offer little to no nutritional value and are very fattening. Instead, drink zero-calorie, 100% healthy water for free.

3. **Eat more beans!** They are cheap, readily available, super-healthy and fantastic for weight-loss because of their high fiber and protein make-up.

4. **Choose walking as your exercise of choice.** A brisk walk provides the full spectrum of health benefits attributed to exercise and is proven to aid in weight-loss. 75 percent of the 4,000+ dieters enrolled in the National Weight-Control Registry Study report walking as an important component of their weight loss success (to be eligible for this study, participants must have maintained a 30 pound weight loss for at least one year).

5. **Eat more fresh produce.** Increasing your consumption of fruits and veggies is a simple and proven means to hasten weight loss. According to a Penn State University Study, people who simply consumed more fruits and veggies lost weight without gimmicks or counting calories. Additionally, a 2004 USDA report found that consuming seven servings of fruits and veggies a day costs as little as 64 cents. The USDA researchers also found that nearly two-thirds of fruits and veggies were least expensive in their fresh form.

[WHAT'S RIGHT FOR LUNCH]

Tuna or Salmon Salad Sandwich

Canned tuna and salmon are exceptional sources of healthy protein. These popular oily fish are perhaps the easiest and most economical way to load up on essential and all-powerful omega-3 fats. For optimal health, everyone should strive for at least three servings weekly of oily fish and this recipe is a tasty way to help you achieve this important nutritional goal. In addition to omega-3 fats, salmon and tuna offer generous amounts of B vitamins and valuable minerals. Moreover, salmon and tuna are two foods that naturally provide the all-star nutrient vitamin D.

Here is how you make this meal…

Ingredients

3–4 ounces of canned tuna or salmon packed in water

1 tbsp red onion, diced finely

2 tbsp chopped celery

1 tsp Dijon mustard or horseradish

1 tbsp canola oil-based or olive oil-based mayonnaise

Lemon juice and pepper to taste

Dark salad greens of choice

2 slices of fresh tomato

2 slices 100% whole wheat or 100% whole grain bread

Directions

Combine the first six ingredients in a small bowl and stir thoroughly. Layer the mixture on one slice of the bread. Top with lettuce, tomato and the other slice of bread.

Dr. Ann's NOTES

➤ There are several lively ways to change up this sandwich. Capers, diced olives and chopped canned artichoke hearts can lend a healthy Mediterranean touch. A dash or two of dried dill, parsley, oregano or curry powder are excellent flavor enhancers. I am especially fond of seasoning my salmon salad with lots of curry powder—try it.

➤ If you want to reduce calories, substitute Greek-style plain yogurt for the mayo.

➤ You will pay a bit more for it, but canned red sockeye salmon has the best flavor (and more omega-3 fat) than the pink varieties.

➤ Canned white Albacore tuna has more omega-3 fat than chunk light tuna, but unfortunately more methyl mercury, too. Women of child-bearing age, teens and children should stick to chunk light tuna.

➤ Double or triple this recipe for quick and easy lunches throughout the week. You can store it in an airtight container in your refrigerator for up to four days

Your Salmon Salad Sandwich Is Packed With Superstar Omega-3 Fats

Superstar Foods:
★ WILD SALMON

Available fresh from early summer to the late fall, usually available frozen, and always available canned—wild salmon is one of the healthiest proteins on earth. This delectable fish is virtually exploding with almighty omega-3 fats along with several key nutrients, including magnesium, selenium, B vitamins, and vitamin D (think heart health, brain health, diabetes protection). Red sockeye is my top pick for flavor and nutritional goodness.

Love Tuna And Salmon? Follow Dr. Ann's Tips On Healthy Seafood Choices

Kitchen Tips:
SEAFOOD

➤ Avoid frying.

➤ Poached, baked, broiled, pan seared, and sautéed are the best ways to prepare seafood.

➤ Take advantage of two superstar sources of omega-3s that are always available and convenient: canned Alaskan salmon and sardines.

➤ Avoid large carnivorous fish (shark, marlin, king mackerel, swordfish, and tilefish). These types of fish may contain unhealthy concentrations of environmental contaminants like PCBs and dioxins.

➤ Choose wild salmon whenever possible. Unfortunately, farm-raised salmon's fatty-acid profile is not as healthy as its wild counterpart. Additionally, it may have unhealthy concentrations of environmental contaminants (PCBs and dioxins).

Sandwiches Are Just The Starting Point Of Increasing Your Whole Grain Consumption

Kitchen Tips:
BREAD

➤ Always have your whole grain bread with some protein or a healthy fat such as olive oil or a slice of avocado. This helps reduce the glycemic response (i.e., your blood sugar level).

➤ Stop serving bread as a routine accompaniment with your meals.

➤ Freshly baked whole grain breads are available in the bakery sections of most grocery stores, and they taste far superior to pre-packaged breads.

Dr. Ann Recommends
GOING "WHOLE" GRAIN

For optimal health and weight, learning how to do your carbs right is one of the most important of all nutritional strategies. A healthy carb diet includes only true, 100% whole grain bread and cereal products, not their refined counterparts. To be sure you are getting a true, whole grain product, you must see "100% whole grain" or "100% whole wheat" on the label or the word "whole" before any grain listed in the ingredients list. If you see "wheat flour" or "enriched wheat flour" on the ingredients list, it is nothing more than white flour disguised as the healthier option. Remember, whole grains have been shown to aid in the maintenance of a healthy body weight and protect overall health, whereas refined grains have been linked to weight gain and an increased risk of some chronic diseases.

[WHAT'S RIGHT FOR LUNCH]
Deli-Style Your Way

The deli sandwich is one of America's most beloved lunches. They are easy and quick to prepare, yet are packed with flavor and nutritional punch. With a little mindfulness in selecting the right ingredients, anyone can construct a delicious and healthy deli sandwich. Every now and then I simply crave a toasted roast beef and Swiss on rye (with a side of chips!). Because I know how to make the necessary healthy tweaks, I can indulge and feel good about it, too.

Here is how you make this meal…

Ingredients

3 ounces deli style turkey, chicken or roast beef (nitrate/nitrite free are best)

1 tbsp canola or olive oil-based mayonnaise

1–2 tsp mustard of choice

1 slice part-skim mozzarella or 2% milk cheddar or Swiss cheese

2 slices 100% whole wheat or 100% whole grain bread

As many and as much a variety of sandwich-friendly veggies as possible

Directions

Spread the mayonnaise over one slice of the bread. Top with deli meat, cheese and any veggies you are adding. Spread the second slice of bread with the mustard and cover the sandwich.

Dr. Ann's NOTES

➤ Many deli meats contain nitrates or nitrites which may come with some health risks, so look for "natural" versions that are nitrate/nitrite free (check ingredients list). Boar's Head® is a popular brand, but others are available. Stay away from processed varieties of deli meat like salami, bologna, pastrami and ham, as they have been repeatedly linked to increased cancer risk, and most recently heart disease and type 2 diabetes.

➤ If you want to cut some calories, substitute plain Greek-style yogurt for the mayonnaise.

➤ To avoid brown-bag boredom—consider alternative spreads like smashed avocado, hummus, horseradish sauce or salsa.

➤ Experiment with different herbs and spices. Garlic powder, oregano, curry powder and dried onion will give your sandwich more zip. You can even tuck in some whole fresh basil leaves for a big flavor blast.

➤ Last but not least, load on those colorful and crunchy veggies! Dark leafy greens, tomatoes, brocco sprouts, bean sprouts, pickles, cucumbers, bell peppers and shredded purple cabbage will keep things balanced and delicious.

➤ And if you love a side of chips like I do, choose a multigrain (like Sun Chips®) or baked variety. I adore the Food Should Taste Good® brand of tortilla chips and they have three grams of fiber *and* protein per serving!

Don't Just Settle For The Same Old Thing:
Use Alternatives For Your Sandwich Bread

Bring More Excitement To
YOUR SANDWICH

To avoid sandwich monotony, you can substitute any of the following for sliced bread: bagels, tortillas, English muffins, wraps, pita pockets, or the new sandwich thins (Arnold®) and deli flats (Pepperidge Farms®). The last two are excellent choices for those trying to cut calories. Just be certain you choose 100% whole wheat or 100% whole grain products.

Make Your Deli-Style Superstar-Style And Take Big Steps To Increase Your Fiber

Superstar Foods: BROCCO SPROUTS

Developed by cancer researchers from Johns Hopkins and now available in the produce aisle of most standard grocers, brocco sprouts are brimming with health-boosting goodness. They contain 20 times more sulforaphane (nature's anti-cancer wonder chemical) than mature broccoli. They also offer a nice dose of fiber, vitamin C and folate. Throw them into your salads or add to your sandwiches. Look for the Brassica® brand for best results.

Superstar Foods: TURKEY

Turkey, especially skinless turkey breast is one of the most nutritious, economical and versatile forms of protein available. This super lean form of animal protein is an excellent source of B vitamins, selenium, and zinc. Three ounces of skinless turkey breast provides 26 grams of protein, 115 calories and just two grams of saturated fat. For perspective, three ounces of extra lean (95%) ground beef provides 22 grams of protein, 145 calories, and 2.4 grams of saturated fat.

[WHAT'S RIGHT FOR LUNCH]

Green Goddess Bean Wrap

This easy to prepare "gourmet" wrap is one of my all time favorite lunches. It hosts a luscious array of flavors, colors, textures and nutritional pop that is sure to please your taste buds along with the rest of your body. And because it features six separate superstar foods, it is likely to improve your health by mid-afternoon.

Here is how you make this meal…

Ingredients

2 cups red cabbage chopped into thin strips

1 medium red bell pepper, diced

¼ cup chopped fresh parsley or cilantro

Juice of ½ lime (more if you like it)

Hot sauce to taste (I use two dashes)

2–3 tbsp seasoned rice vinegar or vinegar of choice

1 ripe avocado

1, 15-ounce can rinsed cannellini or other white beans

2 tbsp red onion, finely diced

½ cup crumbled goat cheese or feta cheese

Salt and pepper to taste

4 100% whole wheat 6–8 inch tortillas

Directions

Combine the cabbage, bell pepper, fresh herbs, lime juice, hot sauce, and vinegar in a bowl. Mash the avocado and beans together in a separate bowl. Stir the cheese and onion into the avocado/bean mixture until thoroughly blended. Spread ¼ of the cheese/avocado/bean mixture onto the center portion of a tortilla and top with ⅔ cup of the cabbage mixture. Roll up the tortilla so the ends are folded in and secured. Repeat with the rest of the tortillas. Wrap the tortillas in foil for safe and easy transport.

Make Your Green Goddess Bean Wrap Shine With Superstar Veggies!

Superstar Foods:
RED BELL PEPPERS

This sweet and refreshing vegetable is definitely the cream of the bell pepper crop. In fact, red bell peppers are one of the most nutrient-dense of all vegetables. A single, half serving provides 140 percent (more than oranges!) of your daily dose of vitamin C, and 50 percent of your daily vitamin A. This gem of a vegetable is also prized for its cancer-fighting lycopene and its vision-protective lutein phytochemicals (green bell peppers don't contain either).

Superstar Foods:
RED ONIONS

Although they quite literally bring us to tears, the organosulfur phytochemicals unique to onions and the other members of the allyl food group (garlic, leeks, chives, and scallions) are truly medicinal in their power to protect our health. Red onions are the true superstar standout of this bunch, however, because they are uniquely high in both quercetin and anthocyanins—two of nature's most remarkable anti-inflammatory agents. Remember, inflammation is a key driver of most chronic diseases. The health benefits of red onions are optimized when they are chopped or sliced and eaten raw or lightly steamed.

The Green Goddess Bean Wrap Is The Path To Getting Your Beans And Legumes

Kitchen Tip:
BEANS & LEGUMES

➤ Although canned beans are just fine, I recommend you develop the habit of preparing dried beans in a pressure cooker. Dried beans are superior in taste, texture, and nutritional value. Most beans can be prepared in 20 minutes or less in the pressure cooker.

➤ Hummus and other bean dips are great for dipping freshly cut vegetables in or using as a mayonnaise alternative in sandwiches/wraps.

[WHAT'S RIGHT FOR LUNCH]

Rice Bowl Delight

NUMBER OF SERVINGS • NUMBER OF SERVINGS

1

My college-age daughter, Liz, who is as much of a foodie and health nut as her mom (and on a super-tight budget!) provided the inspiration for this recipe. The terrific trio of brown rice, beans and vegetables create one of the most satisfying, cost-effective and sinfully nutritious lunches around.

Here is how you make this meal…

Ingredients

1 cup cooked brown rice (Follow package instructions. I prefer mine cooked in chicken broth.)

¾ cup or more mixed veggies of choice—onions, bell peppers, carrots, broccoli, mushrooms, celery, etc.

½ cup of rinsed canned beans of choice

¼ tsp cumin or to taste

¼ tsp garlic powder or 1 clove fresh garlic, minced

¼ cup feta cheese—optional

Directions

In a skillet coated with a teaspoon of extra virgin olive oil, sauté your choice of mixed veggies over medium heat. Cook the veggies until they reach your desired texture (tender, but still crisp offers the most health benefits). Place one cup of cooked brown rice in a medium to large single-serving bowl. Add the sautéed veggies along with the remaining ingredients and stir—enjoy.

Dr. Ann's

NOTES

➤ If you get bored with the brown rice, substitute another whole grain like quinoa (my favorite!), farro, pearl barley or whole wheat cous cous. The cous cous and quinoa cook in 15 minutes.

➤ Virtually any vegetable or vegetables you desire will work—the more the better! If you don't have time to cook fresh veggies, throw in some diced tomatoes, peas and green beans right from the can.

➤ Add a few tablespoons of canned tomato paste or prepared salsa to add flavor, lycopene and fiber.

➤ For those who like savory and sweet, raisins and diced apricots are healthy additions.

➤ For added texture and crunch, toss in a small handful of nuts or seeds.

➤ Do not skip the herbs and spices—they really complete this dish. In addition to cumin and garlic, I encourage you to add any of the following: oregano, paprika, curry, turmeric, chipotle, thyme, ginger, cilantro, basil, dill or celery seed.

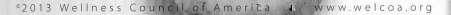

Add The Spices Of Life When You Make Your Next Rice Bowl Delight!

Dr. Ann Recommends
HERBS & SPICES

Get into the healthy habit of adding herbs and spices to your meals and dishes. They contain truly "medicinal" levels of beneficial plant compounds. Think of them as wonder drugs that enhance the flavor of your foods with no side effects! Fresh herbs offer the most flavor and the highest concentrations of phytochemicals, but dry herbs are still plenty powerful.

Make Your Rice Bowl Delight Shine With Dr. Ann's Superstar Foods!

Superstar Foods:
CARROTS

Crunchy, sweet, super low in calories, carrots are an exceptional food. Just a half cup serving provides 340 percent of your day's worth of Vitamin A along with a whopping dose of carotenoid antioxidants. Carrots are also legendary when it comes to disease protection. Enjoy them regularly for heart health, vision protection, blood sugar regulation, optimal lung function, and protection from some cancers.

Superstar Foods:
QUINOA

This ancient whole grain was revered by the Inca's and is arguably the healthiest of all whole grains (technically it is a seed, but we call it a whole grain because of its taste and texture). It is a fantastic source of minerals, fiber, and protein (including all the essential amino acids). It cooks in 15 minutes or less and can be used just as you would rice. Quinoa is a staple in my cupboard. Wholesale grocers carry large bags of organic quinoa that are an excellent value.

Make Health Gains With Whole Grains

Whole Grains Are
GREAT FOR YOU!

Including more whole grains in your diet is one of the tastiest and most effective ways to reduce your risk of heart disease, stroke, type 2 diabetes, many cancers and obesity. For best results, strive for three servings of whole grains every day.

Here are seven easy ways to get three servings a day. One serving is ½ cup prepared whole grains like oatmeal or brown rice; one slice of 100% whole wheat bread; a serving (check the nutrition label) of any 100% whole grain cereal; one ounce of 100% whole grain crackers/snacks.

1. One cup of prepared oatmeal for breakfast; ½ cup brown rice at dinner.

2. A serving of 100% whole wheat/grain cereal for breakfast; a sandwich at lunch made with 100% whole wheat or 100% whole grain bread.

3. One 100% whole wheat bagel at breakfast; one ounce (standard serving) of whole grain tortilla chips for a snack.

4. One-half cup stone ground whole grain grits (not standard grits) at breakfast; one 6" 100% whole wheat tortilla at lunch; ½ cup barley at dinner (great in soups and stews).

5. Three-fourths of a cup prepared oatmeal at breakfast; ¾ cup quinoa at dinner.

6. One-half cup homemade granola (see my recipe on page 39) at breakfast; one serving (one ounce) of 100% whole wheat crackers as a snack (100% whole wheat Wheat Thins®, Ak-Mak®, Rye Crisps®, Triscuits®); ½ cup brown rice at dinner.

7. One 100% whole wheat English muffin at breakfast; ¾ cup quinoa at dinner.

If you want to be adventurous, try the other more exotic whole grains—farro, kamut, spelt, amaranth, triticale and kasha.

If you're diabetic, pre-diabetic, overweight or trying to lose weight, physically intact grains (oatmeal, brown rice, quinoa, etc.) are best. In other words, avoid breads and other flour-based products even if they are made with whole grains.

[WHAT'S RIGHT FOR LUNCH]

Mediterranean Chicken Pita

· NUMBER OF SERVINGS ·
1
· NUMBER OF SERVINGS ·

The healthfulness of Mediterranean cuisine has been repeatedly validated in scientific studies and this pita pocket deliciously taps into the best of this winning style of eating. It features appetite-quieting lean protein, a tasty bouquet of fresh superstar veggies, a generous serving of whole grains and a yummy sauce that is 100% guilt free.

Here is how you make this meal…

Ingredients

3–4 ounces shredded or chopped chicken breast (pre-packaged strips or rotisserie chicken are easiest)

¼ cup canned sliced black olives

¼ cup canned, chopped artichoke hearts

1 large handful of baby spinach leaves

2 tbsp prepared tzatsziki sauce (Greek cucumber sauce available in most grocers)

¼ cup crumbled goat or feta cheese

Several diced cherry or grape tomatoes

1 100% whole wheat pita pocket

Directions

Combine the first seven ingredients in a bowl and mix thoroughly. Slice off the top edge of the pita pocket and carefully open it up. Stuff the mixed ingredients into the pita. Wrap it tightly in foil if you are packing your lunch.

Dr. Ann's
NOTES

➤ Feel free to experiment with the ingredients in this refreshing sandwich. Easy protein stand-ins include: turkey, canned beans, tofu, hummus, or canned tuna or salmon.

➤ As always, any fresh veggie is a go—I love to add shredded purple cabbage, diced red onion and brocco sprouts.

➤ If you can't find tzatsziki sauce, a little olive oil with vinegar or lemon juice will do just fine.

➤ Lastly, open your spice drawer and shake in some powdered garlic, oregano and/or basil.

Make Your Mediterranean Chicken Pita The Right Way: More Spinach And Less Salt

Superstar Foods:
SPINACH

Spinach is a nutrient Goliath—packing in more nutrition per unit calorie then any other food. Spinach's tender green leaves are home to a whopping dose of Vitamins A, C, and K. Spinach is also rich in folate, iron, calcium and zinc. Spinach is one of the richest sources of eye-protective lutein and also provides both alpha-lipoic acid and glutathione—two of the most important antioxidants found in the body.

Cooking diminishes both folate and Vitamin C levels in spinach, but actually increases the bioavailability of carotenoids like beta-carotene and lutein. For this reason, it's best to regularly include both raw spinach and lightly cooked (steamed/stir steamed) spinach in your diet.

Dr. Ann Recommends
NIX THE SALT

Adding salt to prepared food is a learned behavior primarily triggered by seeing and having ready access to a salt shaker. As a simple strategy to reduce your sodium intake, completely rid your house of salt shakers. If it's not there, it is not an option. Americans currently consume 50 percent more salt than we did in the '70s. If every American reduced their salt intake by just one gram a day, (we currently average 10 grams a day) there would be 250,000 fewer new cases of heart disease and more than 200,000 lives saved over a decade.

Going Mediterranean-Style: It's All In The Mix Of Ingredients

Dr. Ann Recommends
GO MEDITERRANEAN!

The "Mediterranean Diet," long touted for its health-protective potential, continues to score one scientific victory after another. In the past two years alone, this delectable eating style has been associated with lower rates of heart disease, type 2 diabetes, metabolic syndrome, Alzheimer's disease, weight gain, skin cancer, and depression. The authentic Mediterranean Diet is rich in fruits, vegetables, whole grains, fish and olive oil and low in red meat, refined carbs, and full-fat dairy products.

Superstar Foods:
TOMATOES

Tomatoes are the most widely consumed non-starchy "veggie" (really a fruit) in America and this is a wonderful thing! Tomatoes offer a treasure chest of nutrients for boosting your health, but their crown jewel is a super potent antioxidant called lycopene. Scientists speculate that tomatoes' rich supply of lycopene is the key factor that makes this veggie a major health win. People who eat the most tomatoes *and* tomato-based products get less prostate cancer, colon cancer, osteoporosis, sun-damaged skin, cardiovascular disease and dementia. Please make note that *processed* tomato products like tomato sauce, paste, or marinara beat out fresh tomatoes in terms of lycopene concentration. This is one of the very rare examples where processed is better for you than fresh! When you choose fresh tomatoes, the smaller the tomato the more concentrated the lycopene. I eat grape tomatoes by the handful!

[WHAT'S RIGHT FOR LUNCH]

Quick Homemade Veggie Pizza

NUMBER OF SERVINGS
1
NUMBER OF SERVINGS

This lunch shatters the myth that eating pizza can't be part of a healthy diet! It also buries the misconception that making homemade pizza is a long and arduous task. Anyone can whip this wholesome pizza up in a flash. My pizza-loving kids were all experts with this recipe (at least through the cheese part) by the age of 12.

Here is how you make this meal…

Ingredients

1, 6–8 inch 100% whole wheat tortilla or 100% whole wheat pita pocket, slightly toasted

2–3 tbsp canned tomato paste (low-sodium is best)

¼ cup shredded part-skim mozzarella cheese or 2% milk cheese

1 cup baby spinach leaves or ½ cup thawed frozen spinach

3 tbsp chopped canned roasted red peppers

1 tbsp pine nuts (optional)

2 tbsp chopped fresh basil leaves

1 clove minced garlic

1 tbsp balsamic vinaigrette (see homemade dressing recipes on page 52)

Directions

Preheat oven to 375 degrees. Spread the tomato paste evenly over the slightly toasted tortilla or pita bread. Top with remaining ingredients in this order: cheese, spinach, peppers, pine nuts, basil and garlic. Drizzle or sprinkle the balsamic vinaigrette evenly over the prepared pizza. Carefully place the pizza on a cookie sheet sprayed with pan spray and place in the oven. Cook until the cheese melts and the spinach (if fresh) wilts (about 7–10 minutes). Let it cool a bit before serving.

Dr. Ann's NOTES

➤ Just like your favorite pizza joint, this recipe comes with a long list of topping choices. As long as you stick with 100% whole wheat crust, you can swap out or add any of the following veggies: tomatoes, onion, bell peppers, broccoli, mushrooms, olives and peas.

➤ If you want a more highly flavored cheese, sprinkle on some feta or goat cheese.

➤ If you dare to be different, which is what I like to do—go 100% green—substitute pesto for the tomato paste and top the cheese with lots of broccoli and spinach.

Super-Charge Your Quick Homemade Veggie Pizza With Garlic!

Superstar Foods:
GARLIC

A recent review of the latest studies evaluating garlic's beneficial effects on blood pressure provided some real artery-opening results. After combining the data from 11 separate clinical trials, researchers found that garlic indeed packs an impressive blood pressure-lowering punch. For folks in the studies who had high blood pressure, the garlic reduced the top (systolic) and bottom (diastolic) numbers by a whopping 8.4 and 7.3 mm Hg, respectively (*BMC Cardiovascular Disorders*, Online, 6-16-08). These results are similar or even better than what we observe with standard doses of blood pressure medications!

The average garlic dose used in these studies was equivalent to one-half to one clove. Because high blood pressure is arguably the single greatest contributor to heart attack risk, I recommend that you get into the habit of using fresh garlic regularly. For best results, chop or mince, let sit for 5-10 minutes and then add to your dishes at the end of cooking. Heat can reduce the effectiveness of garlic's active ingredients.

If You Don't Have Time For This Quick Homemade Veggie Pizza…

Don't Forget…
YOUR LEFTOVERS!

Most of my lunches are dinner leftovers. This tactic saves time and money and because I ALWAYS make a healthy dinner, it guarantees a healthy lunch. Most dishes mature deliciously overnight in the fridge so your taste buds will thank you, too. Just remember that food safety experts recommend you quickly store prepared foods in the fridge and eat them within four days to reduce the risk of food poisoning. Reheat them thoroughly in a microwave oven.

Include Any Of These Great Side Items With Your Lunches

Finger & Desktop-Friendly
LUNCH SIDE ITEMS

- ➤ Grapes
- ➤ Cherry tomatoes
- ➤ Baby carrots
- ➤ Broccoli or cauliflower florets
- ➤ Individual containers of hummus (for dipping your veggies)
- ➤ Fresh blackberries or strawberries
- ➤ Individual containers of low-fat yogurt
- ➤ Nuts
- ➤ Soy nuts
- ➤ Park-skim mozzarella cheese sticks
- ➤ Dark chocolate baking chips (a small handful is a prudent portion)
- ➤ Boiled eggs
- ➤ 100% whole grain crackers
- ➤ Dried apricots
- ➤ Sundried tomatoes

Organic Foods

There has been an explosion in the marketing and availability of organic foods over the past few years, so it's certainly no wonder that one of the most common questions I'm asked is "should I buy organic?"

I'm sure you have probably asked the same question. What follows is the "lowdown on organics." Use this information to make an informed decision that will best serve you and your family.

Here are the facts based on the best science to date:

➤ **Choosing organic is clearly better for the environment.** This occurs through numerous channels, including conservation of natural resources and less pollution for our water and soils.

➤ **Consuming organic foods reduces your exposure to pesticides.** This has been confirmed through numerous scientific studies. Adults and children who consume organic foods have measurably lower levels of pesticides in their bodies. Perhaps the bigger question here is, "Are the levels of pesticides in conventional foods harmful to our health?" At this point in science, we simply do not have the data to definitively answer this question. Pesticides approved for use are reported to be safe at or below certain threshold levels. It is clear, however, that pesticides are harmful to exposed farm workers, along with "non-target" wildlife and are definitely not healthy substances.

For children, there are two additional caveats to consider on the safety front. Because children consume more food calories per unit of body weight and because their cells are dividing at a much more rapid rate, they are at greater risk for potential toxic effects from pesticide exposure (a developing fetus is at the greatest risk). Additionally, it is common for some kids to have very restrictive eating patterns, with consumption of only one or a few types of fruits or vegetables on a regular basis. If this is the case, they will experience a greater number of exposures to the same pesticides, which can also exacerbate risk!

The Environmental Working Group (EWG), a not-for-profit research organization devoted to improving public health and the environment, has determined that the produce that consistently has the highest pesticide levels include: apples, bell peppers, celery, cherries, grapes (imported), nectarines, peaches, pears, potatoes, red raspberries, strawberries, and spinach. Choosing organic for this group of produce will give you and your family the greatest reduction in pesticide exposure. Spinach, strawberries, and celery are the worst of the bunch. I only buy organic in these three varieties of notoriously pesticide-laden foods.

➤ **Organic foods may or may not be more nutritious than their conventional counterparts.** Some scientific studies show conventional foods are just as nutritious, while others support the contrary. Based on the available data, the scale tips very slightly in favor of a superior nutritional profile for organic varieties. Organics generally have a slightly higher mineral content because of more stringent soil requirements for organic certification and in some cases, organics have a more robust supply of protective antioxidants.

➤ **Organic foods may or may not taste better.** Blind taste studies are basically a wash. For those who think organic tastes better, there are an equal number who find the conventional counterpart tastier.

➤ **Organic foods will generally spoil more quickly.** Pesticides clearly extend the shelf life and freshness of foods. For optimal freshness, organic foods should be consumed more quickly.

➤ **Organic foods are more expensive.** You will generally pay about 20% more for organic varieties.

So, you see the answer is a complicated one and ultimately depends on your feelings towards the environment, pesticide exposure, and your pocketbook.

Eat **Right** For Dinner

A

t the end of the day, I think everyone deserves the comfort and pleasure that eating a wholesome, home-cooked meal with loved ones can provide.

With my often hectic work day behind me, I cherish sitting down at the dinner table with my family to enjoy a meal that is nutritious, fresh, flavorful and simple to prepare. Having spent the past 20 years devoted to healthy family dinners, I am delighted to share the following 10 tried-and-true dinner meal plans and recipes. I have made these meals over and over again because they work, my family loves them and they are easy for the cook! All of the dinner meals that follow serve about six people.

[WHAT'S RIGHT FOR DINNER]

Pan-Seared Salmon

with Dr. Ann's Favorite Bean Salad and Roasted Cauliflower

NUMBER OF SERVINGS · NUMBER OF SERVINGS

6

www.welcoa.org ★ ©2013 Wellness Council of America

Dr. Ann's NOTES

consider salmon one of the healthiest proteins available and with this fail-safe recipe anyone can succeed in preparing this delectable fatty fish. In addition to high quality protein, salmon offers a whopping dose of omega-3 fats, along with several important nutrients including selenium and vitamin D. Current health recommendations suggest that you consume at least two servings of fish weekly, so make salmon a regular player at your dinner table.

My favorite bean salad is a delicious accompaniment to the salmon and is exploding with flavor and nutritional goodness. We fight over seconds in my household! It is truly a dish that makes me feel healthier on-the-spot. In fact, this dish is so healthy *and* so tasty that I consider it my all-time favorite dish. I have NEVER served this salad to anyone, including young children, who did not love it.

Here is how you make this meal…

Ingredients & Directions

SALMON

2–2 ½ lbs fresh salmon filet   Bottle of ginger/soy marinade

Put the salmon filet in a large Ziploc® bag with enough marinade to cover. Marinate for about 30-60 minutes in the refrigerator. Spray a large skillet with pan spray and heat to medium/high. Add salmon skin side up and cook for five minutes. Turn filet over, cover and cook at same medium/high heat for about seven minutes until *just* done all the way through. Remove skin before serving.

BEAN SALAD

2 (15–ounce) cans black beans, rinsed   2–3 tbsp seasoned rice wine vinegar
1 small can white corn, rinsed   ½ red onion, finely diced
1 red bell pepper, chopped   1 peeled, seeded cucumber, chopped
1 orange bell pepper, chopped   Juice of 1 lime
2–3 tbsp extra virgin olive oil   1 bunch of fresh cilantro, chopped

Combine beans, corn, bell peppers, cucumbers, red onion, and cilantro in a large, shallow bowl. Add lime juice and drizzle with extra virgin olive oil and vinegar. Stir until combined.

ROASTED CAULIFLOWER

2 heads cauliflower, cut into florets   Extra virgin olive oil   Kosher salt

Put cauliflower florets in a large baking dish. Drizzle with extra virgin olive oil (about two tablespoons) and toss with your fingers until florets are lightly covered in oil. Sprinkle evenly with kosher salt. Roast at 375–400 degrees, turning once until browned (about 25 minutes).

> ➤ Chef Paul Prudhomme's Magic Salmon Seasoning® is a delicious alternative to the ginger/soy marinade. You use it like a rub. You can also roast or grill your salmon if you like. When preparing fresh salmon, it is critical not to overcook it. I like to remove it from the heat when the center still has a touch of a darker pink color.

> ➤ Feel free to change up the ingredients in the bean salad to best suit your palate. Virtually any variety or combination of rinsed, canned beans will work as well as any variety of diced raw veggies. If you don't care for the strong flavor of cilantro, substitute some chopped fresh parsley or any other fresh herb. A dash or more of your favorite hot sauce is fine if you want a bit of a kick. Throw in some diced avocados or diced mangos. And of course be sure to make enough so you have leftovers because the flavor of this dish is even better the next day. I always double the recipe so I can pack it up and roll it into whole wheat tortillas for a quick, tasty and satisfying lunch.

> ➤ Cauliflower is my favorite vegetable to roast. If you want to spice things up, sprinkle it with some curry powder or any other herbs and spices you enjoy. Carrots, sweet potatoes, broccoli, Brussels sprouts and asparagus are wonderful roasted too.

Salmon—Always A Sure Find In Dr. Ann's Deep Freeze…

10 Foods That You Will Always Find
IN DR. ANN'S FREEZER

1. Wild, organic blueberries or mixed berries
2. A variety of bulk raw nuts
3. Various cuts of venison
4. Packaged spinach
5. Packaged peas
6. Packaged shelled edamame
7. Packaged organic chicken breast and thighs
8. Ezekial 4:9® Sprouted 100% Whole Grain Bread
9. 100% Whole Grain Tortillas
10. Packaged Chinese-style vegetables

Beans: Your Superstar Choice For Making Dr. Ann's Favorite Bean Salad

Superstar Foods:
BEANS

Adding beans is a super-quick, convenient, and cheap way to dramatically boost the healthfulness of your meals. Overall, beans have megawatt nutritional power. They provide a healthy dose of appetite suppressive protein and fiber, more folate than any other foods, are rich in minerals, and have potent antioxidant power. Although all beans are great for you, those with the deepest colors are the best choices, including black beans, kidney beans, and lentils.

Make Your Roasted Cauliflower Shine— It's A Superstar Food!

Superstar Foods:
CAULIFLOWER

This savory vegetable is a striking exception to the "white foods are bad for you" rule. Like its cruciferous cousins, broccoli, cabbage, and kale, cauliflower is a nutrition and cancer-fighting powerhouse. Cauliflower provides a hefty dose of fiber, Vitamin C, and folate, but is most prized for its anti-cancer chemicals called glucosinolates and thiocyanates. My family loves it roasted.

Lentils: Another Superstar Legume To Enjoy With Your Meals

Superstar Foods:
LENTILS

Like their bean cousins, lentils are cheap, versatile, filling, and power-packed full of fiber, B-vitamins, protein, minerals, and antioxidant polyphenols. They provide more folate than any other food and have an edge over the other legumes because they cook quickly, require no pre-soaking, and tend to cause less gas.

[WHAT'S RIGHT FOR DINNER]

Dr. Ann's Healthy Spaghetti

with Tossed Salad and Fresh Baked Multigrain Loaf dipped in Extra Virgin Olive Oil

NUMBER OF SERVINGS · 6 · NUMBER OF SERVINGS

I don't think I have ever met anyone who did not love spaghetti. For me, good spaghetti is the quintessential comfort food and this recipe has never let me down. If you are diligent in choosing the leanest forms of ground meat, the healthfulness of this dish will be as supreme as it tastes. Spaghetti is the tastiest way I know to take in a huge dose of the world-famous antioxidant lycopene. Both tomato sauce and tomato paste are amongst the richest sources of this powerful cancer-protective and heart-healthy compound. And because this recipe includes an entire bell pepper, an entire onion, and a full package of mushrooms, you will get a full serving of vegetables in every serving.

Here is how you make this meal…

Ingredients & Directions

SPAGHETTI

1 green or red bell pepper, chopped

1 medium yellow onion, chopped

½ (6-oz) can tomato paste (low-sodium is best)

1 (8-oz) container sliced baby bella mushrooms

1 14.5-oz box multigrain spaghetti noodles

1 lb 96% lean ground beef or ground turkey breast

2 tbsp extra virgin olive oil

1 tsp balsamic vinegar

1 (29-oz) can tomato sauce

2 fresh garlic cloves, minced

¼ cup fresh parsley, chopped

In a large skillet, sauté bell pepper, onion, and mushrooms in extra virgin olive oil until soft. Turn heat up to medium/high and add ground beef or turkey and cook until browned. Stir in tomato paste, tomato sauce, and balsamic vinegar. Bring to gentle boil. Reduce heat, cover and simmer for 10–15 minutes. Stir in garlic and parsley. Serve over spaghetti noodles cooked al dente.

SALAD

Dark salad greens of choice—mixed mesclin, spinach, arugula, bibb, etc. (no Iceberg)

At least four other fresh veggies of choice: carrots, bell peppers, onions, tomatoes, avocado, broccoli, etc.

¼ cup of salad dressing or to taste (see dressing recipes on page 52)

Combine lettuce and veggies in a large bowl. Pour dressing over salad and toss.

MULTIGRAIN LOAF & OLIVE OIL

1 loaf fresh-baked multigrain bread, cut into ½" slices (bakery section of grocer)

Heat bread in oven as desired. Slice and drizzle with a little extra virgin olive oil before serving.

Dr. Ann's NOTES

➤ Feel free to substitute the lean ground beef with ground turkey breast, or ground venison if you like. You can also make this dish fully vegetarian by substituting tofu, tempeh or beans for the meat.

➤ Incorporating additional veggies in this dish is very easy. Excellent choices include shredded carrots or broccoli, baby spinach or finely chopped kale.

➤ If you want to top your spaghetti with some Parmesan cheese (like my kids do)—go for it. Parmesan cheese is loaded with flavor (so a little goes a long way) and provides a respectable dose of calcium.

➤ Cook your noodles al dente (a slightly chewy texture). This will lower their glycemic response, which is better for your metabolism and the health of your arteries.

Maximize Your Family Spaghetti Dinner— Go Multigrain Pasta! Go Multigrain Bread!

Dr. Ann Recommends
MULTIGRAIN PASTA

I recommend you chose a "multigrain" variety. They look and taste like traditional white pasta, but have more fiber and protein (which is fantastic for appetite control and metabolism), along with other key nutrients. I have taste-tested all brands in the standard grocer and Barilla Plus® (yellow box) always comes out on top with my palate. Trust me—your family will never know they are eating healthy pasta.

Dr. Ann Recommends
MULTIGRAIN BREAD

I rarely serve bread with dinner meals, but this is a notable exception. Spaghetti is just not spaghetti without some crusty bread to pair it with. Thankfully, most grocers' bakeries offer a variety of freshly baked whole grain or multigrain breads. Be sure to skip the butter or margarine, and instead drizzle it with a little extra virgin olive oil for some heart-healthy fat, a big hit of anti-inflammatory power and a real Italian touch.

Parsley: Superstar Your Spaghetti Dinner With This Ultimate Flavor Ingredient!

Superstar Foods:
PARSLEY

This refreshing herb provides vitamin A, potassium, calcium, vitamin C and can boast a higher concentration of flavonoids than any other food! Flavonoids are powerful antioxidant and anti-inflammatory compounds that provide cardiovascular protection, cancer protection and hinder the aging process. Tabouli is packed with parsley and Cedar's® or Hannah's® brand tabouli is a staple in my refrigerator. Add chopped parsley to your favorite salads and pastas or go green with your rice dishes by adding a generous portion of chopped, fresh parsley. Like my spaghetti recipe, parsley can dress up almost any main dish.

Grow Your Own
FRESH HERBS

I simply can't say enough positive things about growing your own fresh herbs (or veggies!). I do it and know you can, too. Here are six reasons why you should grow your own herb garden:

➤ **It saves you money.** A package of fresh herbs from the grocer costs $3 to $6 and will typically be enough for just two to three meals. Potted herbs sell for $2 to $4 and can last up to eight months.

➤ **They taste better.** Fresh herbs provide maximum flavor and fragrance when they are cut fresh from the growing plant.

➤ **They are beautiful to look at.** The vibrant green leaves add beauty and tranquility to your surroundings.

➤ **They are super-easy to grow.** All you need is a pot, some potting soil, and a sunny window sill or small sunny spot on your steps or in your yard. Chives, parsley, mint, oregano, thyme, rosemary and basil are amongst the easiest herbs to grow.

➤ **They smell wonderful.** Think of them as an instant source of "at home" aromatherapy. When I am feeling blue, all I have to do is just sniff some fresh thyme or rosemary and my mood is instantly lifted.

➤ **They are kid-friendly.** If you have kids, involving them in the process of growing and harvesting fresh herbs can help them become healthier eaters.

[WHAT'S RIGHT FOR DINNER]

Rotisserie Chicken or Turkey Breast

with Rice and Peas and Steamed Spinach with Feta

NUMBER OF SERVINGS · NUMBER OF SERVINGS ·
6

Honest to goodness, this meal can be prepared in less than seven minutes. This is my go-to-meal when "there is no possible way I can make dinner tonight!" I find grocery store rotisserie chicken delicious (better tasting than what I could bake myself) and consider it a time-saving God-send. I can't count the number of occasions I have literally sprinted into the grocery store on the way home from an unexpected late day (or night) in the office, thrown the wholesome convenience foods featured in this menu quickly into my shopping cart, raced home, and succeeded in putting a hot dinner on the table. With this dinner menu, excuses for no time to prepare a family meal are busted.

Here is how you make this meal…

Ingredients & Directions
CHICKEN/TURKEY
Rotisserie chicken or turkey breast from your grocer's deli section

Slice chicken or turkey breast as desired.

RICE & PEAS
2–3 packages Uncle Ben's® Ready Chicken Whole Grain Rice®
2 (15-oz) cans crowder or field peas

Heat rice in microwave per package instructions. Heat canned peas on the stove and serve over rice.

SPINACH + FETA
3 (9-oz) bags washed, fresh baby spinach leaves (organic is best)
½ cup crumbled feta cheese
Juice of 1 lemon
1 tbsp extra virgin olive oil

Steam fresh spinach in large pot until soft and wilted (3–4 minutes). Drain water, add extra virgin olive oil, feta cheese, and lemon. Mix and serve.

Dr. Ann's NOTES

➤ Uncle Ben's® Ready Rice® comes in a large variety of selections. Be sure to choose the 100% whole grain varieties—it can get tricky so check the label carefully.

➤ I prefer to use canned crowder peas or field peas with this meal, but any canned bean that you like with rice and chicken would do. I am particularly fond of Margaret Holmes® brand of canned beans and peas. Reduced sodium varieties are healthier if available. I usually dump the heated beans on top of the rice.

➤ Frozen spinach is just as healthy as fresh and can be quickly prepared. If spinach isn't popular among your family, other veggies such as fresh steamed broccoli work nicely, too.

Enhance Your Rotisserie Poultry Dish With Nutrient-Packed Brown Rice Vs. White Rice!

Kitchen Tip:
CHOOSE BROWN RICE

Brown rice is a classic example of a physically intact whole grain and a far superior choice than white rice. Unlike its refined white counterpart, brown rice contains a full package of wholesome nutrition. The refining process that turns brown rice into white rice decimates its nutritional value—stripping out 67% of its vitamin B3, 90% of its vitamin B6, 80% of its vitamin B1, half of most of its minerals, and all of its fiber, healthy fats, and phytochemicals. You and your family deserve the best, so always choose brown rice and leave the white rice on the grocery shelf. Par-boiled and converted (Uncle Ben's®) versions of brown rice cook more quickly and have a texture and color similar to white. Try them if you are feeling a bit reluctant to make the switch.

Dr. Ann Recommends
HEALTHY GRILLING

Grilled meat, especially red meat, is a well known source of two cancer-promoting agents, HCA's and PAH's. HCA's develop when the muscle proteins of meats are exposed to high heat. PAH's form in the black, charred outer portions of grilled meats when the surface fat and juices come into direct contact with the flame and smoke.

You can significantly reduce your exposure to these harmful agents by taking any of the following simple steps:

➤ Partially precook your meat in the microwave for two minutes.

➤ Marinate before grilling. Even a quick 30 second submersion in a marinade liquid is helpful.

➤ Add 1–2 tablespoons of dried rosemary to your meat prior to grilling.

➤ Mix some textured vegetable protein (TVP) into your ground meat at a 1:9 ratio.

➤ Avoid "well done" meats and trim away any charred portions before eating.

➤ Flip the meat frequently to keep the internal temperature lower.

➤ Stick with lean cuts and trim away as much visible fat as possible to decrease flare ups from the open flame.

➤ Grill meats as an occasional treat and consume moderate portions when you do.

➤ Enjoy your grilled meat with as many brightly colored fruit and vegetable sides as possible, as they provide healthful compounds that can counteract the harmful effects of PAH's and HCA's.

Picking Up A Rotisserie Bird On Your Flight Home? Make A List…A Healthy List!

Dr. Ann Recommends
A HEALTHY GROCERY LIST

If you want to achieve nutritional excellence and "feel the power" of food, be sure the following foods are regulars on your grocery list:

- Dark lettuce greens (spinach, romaine, etc)
- Dark leafy greens (kale, collards, etc)
- Red onions
- Tomatoes
- Cabbage
- Asparagus
- Sweet potatoes
- Cauliflower
- Melon
- Kiwi
- Pears
- Mushrooms
- Broccoli
- Brussels sprouts
- Red/orange/yellow bell pepper
- All berries
- Apples
- Oranges/any whole citrus
- Red/purple grapes
- Pomegranates
- Any fresh or dried herbs especially—ginger, rosemary, turmeric, curry, garlic
- Plums
- Cherries
- Organic plain soy milk
- Low-fat plain yogurt
- Extra virgin olive oil
- Edamame
- Tofu
- Tempeh
- Oily fish (Wild Alaskan salmon is my top pick)
- Skinless poultry (turkey breast, chicken)
- 100% Whole grain cereals
- Whole oats (steel cut or "old-fashioned" are best)
- Quinoa
- Wheat germ
- Oat bran
- Brown rice
- Wild rice
- Beans/legumes
- Roasted red peppers
- Any form of canned tomato product
- Canned 100% pumpkin
- Beans—any form and any variety
- Green peas (frozen are especially convenient)
- Bagged or loose leaf tea(green or white is best)
- Canned salmon(red sockeye best)
- Hummus/other bean dips
- Salsa
- Tabbouleh
- Guacamole
- Pesto
- Sun-dried tomatoes
- Dark chocolate
- Any nut
- Any seed
- Soy nuts

[WHAT'S RIGHT FOR DINNER]
Chicken Veggie Stir-Fry
with Tossed Salad

S tir-frying is a fast and easy way to tap into the flavor and awesome nutrition a medley of quickly cooked vegetables provides. This traditional Chinese technique can be mastered by anyone and simply involves cooking food rapidly over high heat with a minimal amount of added oil. Convenient, ready-to-cook bags of frozen stir-fry veggies are the starring ingredients in this recipe which, is a winner for your pocketbook, waistline and time. Most brands feature a broad array of superstar veggies including broccoli, carrots, onions and red bell peppers. Toasted sesame oil is the perfect oil for this high heat dish and lends a divine nutty flavor. It also comes along with a nice dose of vitamin E and cholesterol-lowering compounds called phytosterols. In fact, sesame oil is one of the very best sources of this "natural" cholesterol-buster. The brown rice is hearty and filling, and the only type of rice worthy of being a part of a meal with this level of nutritional dignity.

Here is how you make this meal…

Ingredients & Directions

STIR-FRY

2 (6-oz) packages cooked chicken breast strips

About 25 ounces frozen stir-fry veggies (I prefer Kirkland's® brand from Costco®)

2 tbsp canola oil (high heat canola oil is best)

2 tbsp toasted sesame oil

Soy sauce or stir-fry sauce to taste

1 ½ cups brown rice, cooked per package instructions

Heat canola oil and sesame oil in a wok or large skillet over medium/high. Add frozen vegetables, stirring frequently until vegetables are crisp-tender and water is evaporated. Add chicken strips. Stir in soy sauce or stir-fry sauce to taste. Serve immediately over brown rice.

SALAD

Dark salad greens of choice—mixed mesclin, spinach, arugula, bibb, etc. (no Iceberg)

At least four other fresh veggies of choice—carrots, bell peppers, onions, tomatoes, avocado, broccoli, etc.

¼ cup of salad dressing or to taste (see dressing recipes on page 52)

Combine lettuce and veggies in a large bowl. Pour dressing over salad and toss.

Dr. Ann's NOTES

➤ As far as the stir-fry ingredients are concerned, anything goes! Throw in any veggies, fresh or frozen, that you like. Many grocers also carry fresh, bagged precut stir-fry veggies in the produce section. You can use them in lieu of frozen if you prefer. Canned water chestnuts add a great crunch as do any variety of nuts. I love cashews in my stir fry! If you like savory and sweet, mandarin oranges or pineapple tidbits are a colorful addition.

➤ You may also change up the protein—turkey, shrimp, tofu, tempeh or eggs are healthy and delicious substitutions.

➤ Be sure to stir-fry with oil that can stand up well to very high heat. Any oil heated to the point of smoking is filled with unhealthy and toxic compounds—so beware! Grape seed oil and high heat canola oil are two great alternatives to sesame oil.

Make Every Stir-Fry Meal With The Right Ingredients And The Right Pan

Dr. Ann Recommends
GOOD STIR-FRY PANS

The key to good stir-fry is the right pan. A good wok or large, heavy skillet is best. I have both and prefer my large cast iron skillet for my stir-fry's. Be sure to heat the pan before you add the oil to keep the veggies from sticking to it. And use a big enough wok or skillet so the meat and veggies will not be over-crowded. If things get too cramped in the pan, the veggies will steam rather than caramelize, which will diminish their flavor and make them mushy. Continually stirring and keeping the heat high will also help ensure a more flavorful dish.

Superstar Foods:
SESAME SEEDS

Sesame seeds are concentrated nuggets of nutritional excellence. They are exceptionally rich in a host of key minerals, and provide two very special and unique phytochemicals, sesamin and sesamolin. Both are potent anti-oxidants from the lignan family that have been shown to lower cholesterol, prevent high blood pressure, and boost the activity of vitamin E. Throw toasted or raw sesame seeds into your salads, veggies and stir-frys. Keep tahini (pure, ground sesame seeds) as a staple in your fridge and use it in salad dressings and sauces.

Short On Time? Here Is The Perfect Tip For Making Brown Rice Fast…

Kitchen Tip:
QUICKER BROWN RICE

If you don't have time to prepare a regular variety of brown rice, you can get Uncle Ben's® Boil-in-Bag® whole grain rice. It cooks in 8-10 minutes and you will find this version of whole grain rice wonderful. It looks and tastes much like white rice. If 10 minutes is not quick enough for you, Uncle Ben's® also makes a "Ready" line of packaged whole grain rice that cooks in the microwave in 90 seconds.

[WHAT'S RIGHT FOR DINNER]

Black Bean and Cheese Quesadillas

with Broccoli Coleslaw

I love black beans and with this quesadilla recipe going meatless never tasted so good. Canned black beans are a staple in my cupboard because I know they are cheap, convenient, versatile, tasty and exploding with nutritional pop. Black beans house the highest concentration of antioxidant phytochemicals among all beans, which makes them a superstar standout in my kitchen. With the addition of some sautéed veggies, and a bit of cheese layered over a whole wheat tortilla—these quesadillas qualify as a 100% healthy (and delicious) "fast food!"

Convenient packages of "broccoli coleslaw" are now widely available in the produce section of most grocers and are the perfect cheap and healthy companion to many main dishes. Broccoli is home to a spectacular array of health-boosting agents and is widely recognized as one of the most powerful anti-cancer foods. Raw broccoli is even better for you than cooked, and this coleslaw recipe is the most delicious way I have found to include raw broccoli in my family's diet.

Here is how you make this meal…

Ingredients & Directions
QUESADILLAS

1 medium yellow onion, chopped
1 green bell pepper, chopped
1 red or yellow bell pepper, chopped
2 tbsp extra virgin olive oil
2 cloves fresh garlic, minced
1 container reduced-fat sour cream
1 (8-oz) package shredded, part-skim mozzarella cheese

2 (15-oz) cans black beans, rinsed
1 package whole wheat tortillas
1 tsp cumin
Fresh salsa
½ bunch cilantro, chopped
Pan spray

In sauce pan, sauté onions and bell peppers in extra virgin olive oil until soft. Add black beans, garlic, cumin, and cilantro and stir until thoroughly heated. Coat one side of each tortilla with pan spray. Place tortillas coated side down in a skillet over medium heat. Layer bean mixture and then cheese on uncoated side. Top with another tortilla, coated side up. Continue cooking the tortillas in the skillet over medium heat, turning until both sides are lightly brown and toasted. Slice each quesadilla into four pieces and top with sour cream and fresh salsa.

COLESLAW

2 (12-oz) packages broccoli coleslaw
4 tbsp seasoned rice wine vinegar
3 tbsp Hellman's® canola or olive oil mayo

2 tbsp extra virgin olive oil
1 heaping tbsp Dijon mustard

Put broccoli slaw in shallow bowl. Whisk the vinegar, extra virgin olive oil, mayonnaise, Dijon mustard, pour over slaw and toss.

Dr. Ann's NOTES

➤ Feel free to get creative and innovative with this recipe. You can use any variety of canned beans and any combination of sautéed vegetables. Diced carrots, celery, asparagus, mushrooms, and tomatoes are good options. If you want more quick protein, add some diced rotisserie chicken or turkey. Sliced avocados or guacamole are delectable additions as well.

➤ You can do anything you want with herbs and spices. The more you add in terms of variety or quantity, the healthier. In fact, my standard rule with herbs and spices is more, more, more—so add all the cumin and garlic you want!

➤ If you prefer traditional cabbage-based coleslaw—go for it. Cabbage's nutritional goodness rivals broccoli's.

➤ If you are watching your calories, try substituting all or half of the mayonnaise with plain, Greek-style yogurt. Plain, Greek-style yogurt is also a great substitute for sour cream. Try topping off your quesadilla with a spoonful.

Pairing Healthy Fat With Your Vegetables Is A Must

Kitchen Tip:
HEALTHY FAT WITH VEGGIES

To fully leverage all of the glorious goodness in your vegetables—be sure to eat them along with some form of healthy fat. Fat improves their flavor and texture, but most importantly serves as a vehicle for transporting their fat soluble phytochemicals called carotenoids, from the digestive track into the bloodstream. Carotenoids are one of the most revered attributes in veggies. They provide cancer protection, cardiovascular protection and wrinkle-prevention. For goodness sake—do not miss out on all of the carotenoids in your salads by using a fat-free dressing! The healthiest fats to pair with your veggies are extra virgin olive oil, canola oil, nuts, seeds and avocados.

Inject The Best Nutrients Into Your Coleslaw With A Shot Of Broccoli

Superstar Foods:
★ BROCCOLI

Broccoli is one of the healthiest foods on earth. A ½ cup serving provides 20 different essential nutrients and loads of health-boosting plant antioxidants, all for just 22 calories. Hundreds of studies have concluded that broccoli aids in cancer protection, vision protection and heart health. It is simply a no-brainer to include this remarkable vegetable in your diet regularly.

Make Your Quesadillas Totally Homemade: Play Farmer—Grow Your Own Vegetables!

Dr. Ann Recommends
GROWING A GARDEN

I started my garden a few years ago after visiting an incredible farmer's market in Missoula, Montana. Seeing a group of proud locals standing beside a beautiful wealth of produce, inspired me to grow my own crops. Today, my garden provides far more than a bounty of nutritious and wildly delicious vegetables. My garden also gives me the benefit of working outside; I can reconnect with nature, and get some physical activity and Vitamin D. It also allows me to spend some quality time with my family. Even planting a single pot of herbs is a step in the right direction!

[WHAT'S RIGHT FOR DINNER]

Homemade Chicken Noodle Soup

with Pumpkin Cornbread and Just Greens Salad

NUMBER OF SERVINGS
6
NUMBER OF SERVINGS

Sunday night soup is a standard tradition in my home and this recipe is a family favorite. Homemade chicken soup is food for the body and soul—it will warm you inside and out! And with the time-saving use of a grocery store rotisserie chicken, you can prepare this recipe, soup-to-bowl, in under 30 minutes.

The moist and slightly sweet pumpkin corn bread pairs perfectly with this soup, and thanks to canned pumpkin's big umph of nutritional wow, it is great for you too. Canned pumpkin is an under-utilized, under-appreciated, dirt-cheap superfood that is turbo-charged with health-boosting plant compounds called carotenoids. I am always looking for opportunities to add canned pumpkin to my diet because I know how valuable carotenoids are for disease protection and for keeping my skin youthful. Pumpkin corn bread is definitely one of the tastiest ways I have discovered, and my family loves it, too.

Because it's always best to include both cooked and raw veggies, I like to round things off nutritionally with a simple green salad.

Here is how you make this meal…

Ingredients & Directions

SOUP

1 large yellow onion, chopped

3 large carrots, diced

3 stalks celery, chopped

3 tbsp extra virgin olive oil

2 tbsp fresh thyme, chopped

½ box Barilla Plus® penne pasta, cooked per package directions

1 rotisserie chicken, skin removed

2 (32-oz) cartons of chicken broth

½ 28-oz bag frozen peas

½ bunch fresh parsley, chopped

2 cloves fresh garlic, chopped

In a large stock pot, sauté onions and celery in extra virgin olive oil until tender. Pull as much chicken from bone as possible and add to pot with any drippings from bottom of rotisserie container. Add carrots and broth. Bring heat up to boil. Cover, reduce heat to simmer/low and cook for about seven minutes until carrots are tender/crisp. Add frozen peas, parsley, garlic, thyme, cooked pasta and salt/pepper to taste. Stir and serve once peas are heated through.

CORNBREAD

1 ½ cups corn meal mix of choice

3 tbsp canola oil

1 omega-3 egg

¾ cup 1% milk

⅓ can 100% pumpkin (Libby's®)

3 tbsp maple syrup

Preheat oven to 400 degrees. Coat an 8" to 10" skillet or shallow baking dish with pan spray. Combine all ingredients in a mixing bowl and stir until combined. Pour into the skillet or pan and bake until golden brown, about 20–25 minutes.

SALAD

Spring mix or baby romaine greens

Choice of homemade dressing (see dressing recipes on page 52)

Place salad greens in a large bowl. Pour dressing over greens and toss.

Dr. Ann's NOTES

➤ I consider this "the basic chicken soup recipe" which means you have opportunity to alter it as you deem best. Almost any fresh or frozen vegetable can be added to this soup. In fact, feel free to use up any vegetables that are starting to get wilted or tired. I am especially fond of adding chopped kale. You can slip this wonderfood past any finicky eater with this sly technique.

➤ Be sure to choose a multi-grain form of pasta (I prefer Barilla Plus®) for its superior nutritional profile and cook it al dente so it won't get mushy when you add it to the soup.

➤ You can easily substitute rotisserie turkey breast for the chicken.

➤ For a simple green salad, I enjoy getting a packaged spring mix or baby romaine mix. You can use any dark leafy greens that you like, but remember that Iceberg doesn't count. And because there are never any quantity limits on vegetables (other than white potatoes) feel free to add them to your heart and palate's desire.

Live Life: The Eat Right For Life® Scorecard!

	SUN	MON	TUE	WED	THU	FRI	SAT
Minimize/Restrict Great White Hazards—White flour products, white rice, white potatoes, and sugar/sweets.							
5 or more servings of veggies (about 3 cups total)—Best are any dark leafy greens/lettuce, cabbage, broccoli, cauliflower, Brussels Sprouts, carrots, sweet potatoes, onions, garlic, leeks, tomatoes, asparagus, red/orange/yellow bell peppers (limit white potatoes).							
2 or more servings of fruit (about 1 cup total)—Best are berries (any variety) cherries, plums, apples, any whole citrus, cantaloupe, peaches, apples, pears, red grapes, kiwi, avocado, dried or fresh apricots (if overweight or diabetic limit to 2 fruits and avoid dried fruit).							
No sweet beverages—Soda, fruit drinks, fruit juice, sports drinks (choose water [best], unsweetened tea, vegetable/tomato juice, skim milk, soy milk, or coffee).							
At least 1 serving (½ cup) of beans/legumes—Any variety in any form – canned, fresh, frozen, or dried.							
2 –3 servings (½ cup) of 100% whole grains—Intact grains like brown rice, oatmeal, or high fiber cereals are a better choice than whole grain breads.							
Protein at every meal—Best are fish (especially oily fish like salmon, lake trout, sardines, tuna), shellfish, poultry, nuts/seeds, soy, wild game, low fat dairy products, beans, omega-3 eggs (limit red meat and whole dairy products to 2 servings each or less per week).							
Healthy fat at every meal—Best are extra virgin olive oil, canola oil, nuts/seeds, nut butters, avocado, healthy margarine spreads like Smart Balance (avoid butter, stick margarine, shortening, and vegetable oils).							
A small handful (1 ounce) of nuts—Almonds, walnuts, cashews, pistachios, hazelnuts, Brazil nuts, pecans, pine nuts, peanuts (seeds are excellent too).							
Three meals and a mid-afternoon snack							
Portion control—At meals, limit what you eat to what fits into your two hands cupped together. This does not apply to fruits and veggies; there is no need to limit your veggie and fruit intake.							

This Soup Is Great For You And Will Really Fill You Up!

Expect Food To
SATISFY YOU

If you expect a food or meal to satisfy you—chances are it will. Fascinating new research recently presented at a scientific meeting on eating behavior found that our minds can indeed convince our stomachs that a food or meal will fill us up.

Appetite control is critical for achieving a healthy body weight so I encourage you to take advantage of this mind over body reality.

Here is my list of superstar foods for appetite control.

➤ **Healthy animal proteins**—fish, shellfish, skinless poultry, omega-3 eggs, low-fat dairy products (especially plain Greek yogurt).

➤ **Plant proteins**—whole soy foods, nuts, seeds, and beans (especially beans!).

➤ **Non-starchy veggies**—cabbage, kale, broccoli, cauliflower, Brussels sprouts, collards, carrots, onions, leeks, tomatoes, asparagus, spinach, dark lettuces, bell peppers, avocados.

➤ **Mushrooms.**

➤ **Non-tropical fruits**—berries, cherries, plums, apples, pears, grapes, kiwi, peaches, and melon.

➤ **Physically intact whole grains**—oats, brown rice, barley, bulgur, quinoa and kasha etc.

➤ **High fiber cereals**—choose those with at least five grams of fiber per serving (avoid those with more than 10 grams of sugar).

Peas: The Antioxidant Superpower!

Superstar Foods:
PEAS

This diminutive legume is surprisingly powerful on the nutrition front. It is home to a full package of minerals, a big dose of hunger-fighting fiber and protein and scores of vitamins. Scientists have just recently learned that green peas also contain a unique assortment of powerful antioxidant and anti-inflammatory compounds that show great promise for general health protection. Frozen peas (I love the baby ones!) are super convenient and cook-up in three minutes. I regularly add them to my soups, stews, rice dishes and salads.

[WHAT'S RIGHT FOR DINNER]
Chicken Sausage and Asparagus
over Brown Rice with Steamed Broccoli

NUMBER OF SERVINGS
6

www.welcoa.org ★ ©2013 Wellness Council of America

Sausage is a favorite for many, and with this recipe you can indulge without the guilt. Several brands of wholesome, fully-cooked chicken sausage are now available in the grocery store. Contrary to their traditional counterparts made from beef and pork, chicken sausage has far fewer calories and much less fat. This super-simple and speedy dish tastes divine and is always a big hit with my family. I always keep a package or two of chicken sausage in my fridge for those times when I want a really flavorful meal that can be prepared quickly.

Here is how you make this meal…

Ingredients & Directions

SAUSAGE + ASPARAGUS + RICE

12 oz precooked chicken sausage, diced (Casual Gourmet®, Aiddell's®, Al Fresco®)

1 medium yellow onion, chopped

3 tbsp extra virgin olive oil

2 cloves garlic, minced

1 ¼ cups brown rice (cooked according to package instructions)

2 bunches asparagus, ends removed and chopped into two-inch pieces

2 tbsp fresh basil, chopped

½ cup chicken broth

2 tbsp fresh parsley, chopped

Sauté diced sausage in a skillet over medium/high heat until browned. In a separate large skillet, sauté the onion in extra virgin olive oil until soft, stirring occasionally. Add the asparagus and cook over medium/high heat, stirring frequently until asparagus are tender/crisp. Add sausage, chicken broth, garlic, and salt and pepper to taste. Reduce heat and stir until heated through. Add fresh herbs and serve over brown rice.

BROCCOLI

1 large bunch broccoli, cut into florets

Juice of a lemon

2 tbsp Smart Balance Butter Blend® or extra virgin olive oil

Steam broccoli florets in a small amount of water until tender-crisp. Drain. Add lemon juice, Smart Balance or extra virgin olive oil, salt and pepper and toss until florets are coated.

Dr. Ann's NOTES

➤ You have lots of leeway with this main dish. If asparagus doesn't suit you or your family, substitute diced fresh green beans or frozen peas. I also love Brussels sprouts sliced in half and mixed into this dish with or without the asparagus. For a dash of color and even more nutrients, throw in some diced bell peppers of any hue. For a more creamy consistency you can add a few tablespoons of Greek-style plain yogurt or a half cup of evaporated 1% milk at the end of cooking.

➤ The basmati variety of brown rice is the most aromatic and flavorful. This "gourmet" brown rice may cost a bit more, but is well worth it in my opinion. If you have a wholesale grocer nearby (Sam's® or Costco®) you can frequently find organic varieties of brown basmati rice in bulk that is much gentler on your pocketbook. I buy the six-pound container from my local Costco®, and it is a staple in my cupboard. You will not find any white rice in Dr. Ann's kitchen! Keep the Uncle Ben's® Boil-in-Bag® brown rice in mind as a fantastic "bridging strategy" for making the switch from white to brown rice. This is how I succeeded in bringing my four kids into the healthy world of brown rice only.

➤ Although I think broccoli and chicken are a yummy flavor duo—substitute any veggie your family prefers. A tossed salad would go nicely too.

Spice Up And "Winterize" Your Chicken Sausage And Asparagus Meal

Dr. Ann Recommends
HERBS & SPICES

Get into the healthy habit of adding herbs and spices to your meals and dishes liberally and often. They contain truly "medicinal" levels of beneficial phytochemicals that have zero side effects. Fresh herbs offer the most flavor and the highest concentrations of phytochemicals, but dry herbs are still plenty powerful.

Don't Miss Out On The
WINTER SUPER FOODS

Broccoli

Like other non-starchy vegetables, broccoli is filled with health promoting vitamins, minerals, and fiber. It is naturally low in calories and contains over 150 health promoting phytochemicals, including sulforaphane, now famous for its potent cancer protective powers.

Servings—I recommend everyone consume at least one cruciferous veggie daily. Broccoli is certainly one of the healthiest of the bunch. One-half cup is a serving.

Oranges

This refreshing fruit is a great source of vitamin C, folate, and fiber—a terrific trio for heart health. In addition, this special food contains every known class of natural anticancer compounds, making them nature's perfect "anticancer package."

Servings—I recommend that everyone consume a piece of citrus daily. Any citrus will do, but oranges are the superstars.

Kale

All non-starchy vegetables are nutritional treasures, but Kale is the crown jewel. This dark leafy green is without a doubt one of the healthiest foods you can eat, providing more nutrition per unit calorie than any other food. Kale tops the list of the most potent antioxidant vegetables and provides 17 essential nutrients, including 100% of the adult RDA for vitamin A and vitamin C in a single serving. It is an especially rich source of the phytochemicals lutein and zeaxanthin, now famous for promoting eye and vision health. When I feel the urge to "feel" the nutritional power of food, I eat a large plate of sautéed fresh kale.

There Are Plenty Of Other Healthy Food Substitutes!

Dr. Ann Recommends
HEALTHY SUBSTITUTES

Here are some of my favorite healthy substitutions:

➤ 100% spreadable fruit for regular jelly/jams

➤ Trans fat free spreads for stick butter or margarines

➤ Part-skim or 2% cheeses for full fat varieties

➤ Omega-3 fortified eggs for standard eggs

➤ Romaine hearts for iceberg lettuce

➤ Ground turkey breast for ground beef

➤ Greek-style plain yogurt for sour cream

➤ Quaker Oatmeal® pancake mix for regular varieties

➤ Coconut oil instead of shortening for fried chicken

➤ Pureed dates instead of sugar in baking

➤ Coconut milk for heavy whipping cream in recipes

➤ Pureed prunes (baby food) for oil in baking muffins

[WHAT'S RIGHT FOR DINNER]

Portobello & Beef Patty Melt

with Baked Sweet Potato Fries and Homemade Coleslaw

NUMBER OF SERVINGS
6
NUMBER OF SERVINGS

When I'm craving a burger and fries, this meal is my savior! And it is always a winner, even with starving teenage boys post soccer practice. Thankfully with just a few clever tweaks, you can turn a lean patty of ground beef into a flavorful bonanza that will truly melt in your mouth. Portobello mushrooms are the secret weapon in this recipe. They lend a rich, savory flavor and keep the patty moist and juicy. They also provide a wealth of minerals, antioxidants, and immune-boosting chemicals. You and your family will never know you are eating real health food. And because we are on such a positive nutritional roll with this meal—we use sweet potatoes instead of white potatoes for the fries. Spiced, oven-roasted sweet potato fries are brimming with potent carotenoid nutrients and healthy fiber that put the standard deep-fried white potato fries to shame. The crunchy and refreshing coleslaw is chock-full of nourishment too. Truth be told, with this open-face "burger" meal you can really get three servings of veggies at dinner!

Here is how you make this meal…

Ingredients & Directions

PATTY MELT

About 1 ¼ lbs extra lean ground beef
2 large Portobello mushroom caps, chopped
½ yellow onion, finely diced
4 tbsp bread crumbs
1 ½ tbsp Worcestershire sauce

½ tsp kosher salt
½ tsp pepper
2 cloves garlic, minced
6 slices, 100% whole grain bread
6 slices 2% milk Swiss cheese

Combine beef, mushrooms, yellow onion, bread crumbs, Worcestershire sauce, garlic, and pepper in a bowl and mix until just combined. Form into six large, flat patties. Over medium/high heat, cook the patties in a skillet coated with pan spray until browned on both sides and cooked through. Toast bread. Place each patty on a slice of toast, top with cheese and place in oven on broil until cheese melts (about 60 seconds).

SWEET POTATO FRIES

4 large sweet potatoes
Extra virgin olive oil

Kosher salt
1 tsp powdered garlic

½ tsp ground cinnamon
½ tsp cumin

Wash sweet potatoes. Slice diagonally into thick wedges. Cover with a thin coating of extra virgin olive oil. Combine spices and then sprinkle over sweet potatoes. Transfer sweet potatoes in a single layer to a baking sheet. Bake at 450 until tender and golden brown (about 25 minutes). Cool before serving.

COLESLAW

2 (10-oz) packages fresh coleslaw
4 tbsp seasoned rice wine vinegar
2 ½ tbsp canola or olive oil mayonnaise

½ tbsp Dijon mustard
2 tbsp extra virgin olive oil

Put prepackaged fresh coleslaw in a shallow bowl. Whisk together vinegar, mayo, Dijon mustard, and extra virgin olive oil. Pour over coleslaw and toss.

Dr. Ann's NOTES

➤ Add some healthy decadence to this burger by sautéing some thinly sliced onions and peppers and crown the patty with them. You can keep things traditional with toppings of sliced tomato and lettuce or go Tex-Mex with some salsa and sliced avocado. Be sure to use 100% whole wheat or 100% whole grain bread.

➤ Spice up the sweet potato fries as you like. You have so many options—they are great with cayenne pepper, chili pepper, onion powder, ground coriander, cinnamon, nutmeg, powdered ginger, dried oregano, or ground fennel. To ensure a crispy outer layer—try not to over crowd the potato slices. It can also be helpful to turn them midway through the cooking process. And don't peel the potatoes because the skins are loaded with nutrients. I love dipping my sweet potato fries in horseradish sauce—try it!

➤ I love the time-saving convenience of pre-packaged coleslaw. Of course, you can also chop up your own slaw from a head of cabbage, which is a less expensive alternative. When I am in my "chopping mood" (which is usually when I am stressed) I love to make this recipe with a head of red cabbage. The contrast of the purple cabbage with the orange of the fries is visually stunning. I favor the hint of sweet in the seasoned rice vinegar, but any vinegar can work with coleslaw.

➤ Remember, you can always substitute Greek-style plain yogurt for part or all of the mayonnaise to reduce calories and bump up the protein.

Veggie-Up Your Patty Melt With A Tasty Side Of Broccoli

Getting The Most From
BROCCOLI

To take full advantage of broccoli's powerful cancer-fighting compound, sulforaphane, eat it raw, lightly cooked (steam two to four minutes), or pair it with some mustard, arugula, radishes, brocco sprouts or wasabi. All of these simple strategies boost the formation and absorption of the "active" form of sulforaphane. It only takes three to five weekly servings of broccoli to reap its cancer-protective benefits!

You Want Fries With That? The Shining New Superstar Food—Sweet Potato Fries!

Superstar Foods:
SWEET POTATOES

Savory, yet sweet—naturally low in calories, yet filling (because of their super-high fiber content)—sweet potatoes are exploding with immune-boosting, cancer-fighting goodness. They are an excellent source of vitamin C and nature's very best source of beta-carotene. One baked sweet potato provides 250% of our daily requirement for this important nutrient! Because of their fiber-rich make-up, they will not spike your blood glucose levels like regular baked potatoes.

 www.welcoa.org   ★   ©2013 Wellness Council of America

Protein And High-Fiber Are Only A Few Of The Many Metabolism Boosters

How To Boost
YOUR METABOLISM

Even small amounts of excess body fat (especially if deposited in the belly) can boost your risk for several chronic diseases. Simple strategies to power up your metabolism can be very healthful. Simply stated—your metabolism is how many calories you burn for the production of energy required to keep your body functioning properly.

Whether you are trying to lose a few pounds or keep the scale steady—here are some super-easy steps for revving up your metabolism.

1. **Have a cup of green tea.** This is the only indulgence I know of that can boost your immunity, reduce your cardiovascular risk, and bump up your metabolism all for zero calories! For best results, drink regularly and often.

2. **Eat.** Commit to three meals a day with a mid-afternoon snack to keep ravenous hunger at bay. Believe it or not, every time you eat your metabolism jumps up a bit. Skipping meals, especially breakfast, is a known drain for your metabolism and will sabotage your weight loss efforts.

3. **Eat your omega-3s.** Omega-3 fats play a crucial role in maintaining optimal fat-burning potential. Include oily fish (salmon, tuna, sardines), omega-3 fortified eggs, walnuts, dark leafy greens, and whole soy foods in your diet regularly.

4. **Give your metabolic machinery an oil change.** Avoid saturated fats (fatty red meat, butter, whole dairy products) and trans fats (processed foods containing partially hydrogenated oils, shortening, stick margarine). Both tend to slow down your fat-burning engine. Choose the make-me-healthier and leaner monounsaturated fats instead (olive oil, avocados, nuts and canola oil). These fats keep your metabolic machinery operating smoothly.

5. **Steer clear of the Great While Hazards.** This includes white flour products, white rice, white potatoes, and sugar. These foods lead to rapid surges in blood glucose that stress out and overwhelm your metabolic engine. Over time, these foods basically wear things out. They also increase your appetite, providing a real double-whammy.

6. **Get hot!** Super-hot foods like chili peppers, hot mustards, and Tabasco® have been shown to provide a temporary burst in metabolism, along with a subtle mental lift.

7. **Move.** Physical activity helps maintain and can even build lean body mass (muscle). The more muscle you have, the faster your metabolism. In fact, your muscles are responsible for burning about 70% of the calories that you consume.

8. **Get your beauty rest!** Sleep deprivation revs up your appetite-stimulating hormones and leads to a sluggish metabolism. It also zaps your energy, which means you are less likely to move.

[WHAT'S RIGHT FOR DINNER]

Southern Shrimp and Grits

with Tossed Salad and Fresh Baked Multigrain Loaf

As a born and bred southerner whose ancestors all hail from the coast of South Carolina, I am certain the southern culinary tradition of shrimp and grits is in my blood. Shrimp and "hominy," as I was reared to say, is one of my family's most beloved foods. Grits are simply dried corn that has been ground into small pieces, but their nutritional attributes are mighty. Grits provide a respectable amount of protein, a big dose of folate, several minerals, and are surprisingly rich in antioxidants including lutein—an important nutrient for vision preservation. The shrimp are swimming with some vitally important nutrients too, including the terrific trio of B vitamins, omega-3 fats and vitamin D. This meal sings heart and brain health with the warm and friendly twang of a real southern accent!

Here is how you make this meal…

Ingredients & Directions

SHRIMP

½ green bell pepper, finely chopped	1 tbsp Worcestershire sauce
1 small yellow onion, finely chopped	2 cloves garlic, minced
3 tbsp extra virgin olive oil	1 bay leaf
1 ½ lbs fresh or frozen, peeled shrimp	3 tbsp ketchup
1 tsp Dijon mustard	Juice of ½ lemon

In a large skillet, sauté the bell pepper and onion in extra virgin olive oil until tender. Add shrimp and cook over medium/high heat, stirring until shrimp are pink (about 4–5 minutes). Reduce heat to low. Add Worcestershire sauce, garlic, bay leaf, ketchup, lemon juice, and mustard. Stir, cover, reduce heat and simmer for seven minutes. Serve immediately over grits.

GRITS

⅓ stick Smart Balance®	1 cup stone-ground grits	2 tsp kosher salt
2 cups 1% milk	2 cups water	

In a heavy sauce pan sprayed with pan spray, heat two cups of water and two cups of milk to a boil. Add the salt. Slowly add grits—whisking constantly with a wire whisk. Bring back to a boil. Cover, reduce heat, and simmer, whisking every five minutes until cooked (about 25 minutes). Add additional milk as needed for desired consistency and ground pepper to taste.

SALAD

Dark salad greens of choice—mixed mesclin, spinach, arugula, bibb, etc. (no Iceberg)

At least four other fresh veggies of choice—carrots, bell peppers, onions, tomatoes, avocado, broccoli, etc.

¼ cup of salad dressing or to taste (see dressing recipes on page 52)

Combine lettuce and veggies in a large bowl. Pour dressing over salad and toss.

MULTIGRAIN LOAF & OLIVE OIL

1 loaf fresh-baked multigrain bread, cut into half-inch slices (look in the bakery section of grocery)

Heat bread in oven as desired. Slice and drizzle with a little extra virgin olive oil before serving.

Dr. Ann's NOTES

➤ Add a bit of healthy green and some additional flavor to this dish by sprinkling on some chopped fresh parsley, scallions or chives.

➤ You can prepare your grits in four cups of water versus two cups of water and two cups of milk to reduce calories, but it will be less creamy. If you want to go the other way and splurge (occasionally fine!), substitute one cup of half and half for one cup of the 1% milk. You can add flavor to the grits with no added calories by substituting chicken or vegetable broth for the plain cooking water as another option. I strongly recommend that you use some brand of stone ground grits in lieu of the instant variety. It just ain't the same otherwise. My favorite brand is Hagood Mill®. You can order it online if needed at foodforthesouthernsoul. com. As its deeper color suggests, yellow grits have significantly more lutein than white grits.

➤ Because the shrimp and grits are a bit anemic in terms of veggies—be sure to pair this main course with a big robust, colorful side salad.

➤ The bread is optional (always is!), and if you choose to include it, go for the whole grain varieties now available in the bakery section of your grocery store.

Shrimp: Make Your Grits Shine With This Superstar Food!

Superstar Foods:
SHRIMP

Like other shellfish, shrimp offers a delectable and highly nutritious alternative to meat proteins. Shrimp is low in calories and saturated fats and brimming with nourishment including B vitamins, vitamin D and a very respectable dose of omega-3 fats. They are rich in an array of important minerals including zinc, selenium, copper, iron and magnesium and contrary to popular belief, shrimp do not have adverse effects on overall cholesterol levels. In fact, eating shellfish has been shown to actually benefit cardiovascular health, especially when eaten in lieu of fatty red meats.

Dr. Ann Recommends
TWO-FOR-ONE

Because they are so good for you and so tasty—I am wildly enthusiastic about eating lots of salads and want you to eat more of them, too. When you make your salad at dinner, (which is something you should do regularly) go ahead and make one for your lunch the next day. I can tell you from lots of personal experience—this is a huge time saver. It also helps build a habit that is guaranteed to improve your health and save you money!

www.welcoa.org ★ ©2013 Wellness Council of America

Dr. Ann Recommends Including Veggies In All Your Meals

Getting The Most From
YOUR VEGGIES

➤ Choose vegetables with the deepest, richest color. The more color, the more beneficial phytochemicals it provides and usually the more fiber, vitamins and minerals, too. The superstars include: broccoli, cabbage, cauliflower, Brussels sprouts, kale, collards, carrots, garlic, onions, leaks, sweet potatoes, dark leafy greens, tomatoes, winter squash, asparagus, and red/orange/yellow bell peppers.

➤ Some vegetables are better for your raw while others are better for you cooked. Your best bet is to eat some of both every day.

➤ The smaller the piece of produce, the higher its skin to flesh ratio. The nutritional goodness in produce, especially the phytochemicals and fiber, are more concentrated in the skin.

➤ Go for non-starchy vegetables over fruit, especially if you have a weight issue. They have a higher nutrient to calorie ratio and more favorable effects on metabolism.

➤ Seek out locally or regionally grown produce in the grocer. It is generally fresher, tastier, healthier and less stressful on the environment.

➤ Be aware of the vegetables that provide the highest levels of pesticide exposure—spinach, celery, potatoes and sweet bell peppers. I suggest organic for these vegetables.

➤ Be aware of the "cleanest" (least pesticides) vegetables—onions, avocado, frozen corn, frozen peas, asparagus, cabbage, sweet potatoes, and eggplant.

➤ Recognize that frozen vegetables are just as nutritious as fresh.

➤ Try growing your own veggies. Anyone can grow lettuce in a pot.

➤ Eat salad at least once a day. You should never go a day in your life without eating some form of dark leafy green.

➤ Restrict the starchy, higher glycemic vegetables—white potatoes, parsnips, rutabagas and corn.

Asian Chicken Salad

NUMBER OF SERVINGS · NUMBER OF SERVINGS
6

When I need to break out of a dinner rut and reinvigorate my passion for preparing healthy, delectable meals, this one always does the trick. It hosts a bounty of vivid, yet opposing flavors and textures that are simply scrumptious. You get some spicy, sharp, snappy, crunchy and smooth zing in each and every bite. And it is as steeped in nutritional excellence as it is flavorful intrigue. Perhaps the best part of this breaking-out-of-blahdom dinner is that there is no cooking and no clean up. You can prepare and serve this entire meal in a single bowl! It involves lots of chopping too, which is a good thing because as I have learned from years of experience, chopping is a form of culinary meditation. It definitely relaxes me.

Here is how you make this meal…

Ingredients

6 cups chopped Bok Choy or Napa cabbage

1 peeled, seeded cucumber, chopped

½ red onion, finely diced

½ bunch cilantro, chopped

3–4 tbsp. mint, chopped

Juice of 2 limes

3 tbsp reduced-sodium soy sauce

3 tbsp roasted sesame oil

3 tbsp canola oil

5 tbsp seasoned rice wine vinegar (or more to taste)

¾ cup toasted slivered almonds

4 tsp honey

1 ½ cups frozen edamame, cooked as per package instructions

2 (6-oz) packaged cooked chicken breast strips

Directions

Combine all ingredients and gently toss until well-blended. Top with chicken strips and serve.

Dr. Ann's NOTES

➤ This one-dish meal allows for ample versatility. Add any diced raw veggie you like—celery, bell peppers, radishes, carrots and broccoli are fair game. You can definitely use regular green or red cabbage, too.

➤ If you enjoy more sweet with your savory, try some diced apples, pears, mango or mandarin oranges slices.

➤ Heat it up a notch or two with minced ginger or red pepper flakes.

➤ Feel free to substitute the almonds with any nut you prefer.

➤ Play around with the protein by substituting any canned beans for the edamame. Turkey, tofu or tempeh can be excellent replacements for the chicken. Diced rotisserie chicken is a handy alternative to the packaged chicken strips.

Cooked Or Uncooked, Make Dr. Ann's Asian Chicken Salad A Veggie Explosion!

Eat Your Veggies!
RAW AND COOKED

Some vegetables are better for you raw, while others are better for you cooked. Your best bet is to include some of both each day. I strive to include at least one cooked vegetable and one raw variety or varieties as part of my family's dinner each night.

Pesticides Worry You? Use These "Clean 12" Fruits And Veggies In Your Meals!

Minimize Your Exposure To
PESTICIDES

If you are interested in lowering your exposure to pesticides, but find it financially difficult to go the organic route, take note of the "cleanest 12" below. These foods provide negligible pesticide exposure.

- ➤ Onion
- ➤ Avocado
- ➤ Frozen sweet corn
- ➤ Pineapple
- ➤ Mango
- ➤ Frozen sweet peas
- ➤ Asparagus
- ➤ Kiwi
- ➤ Bananas
- ➤ Cabbage
- ➤ Broccoli
- ➤ Eggplant

www.welcoa.org ★ ©2013 Wellness Council of America

Salads And Vegetables Are The Real Thing, But Be Wary Of Foods In Disguise…

Foods You Think Are Healthy, But Are Really…

HEALTH IMPOSTERS

1. **Flavored Yogurt Products:** Although these "healthy favorites" provide some calcium, B vitamins, and essential amino acids, they are loaded with added sugar—in many cases more than is typically found in a standard dessert. "Yogurt" products, through slick packaging and clever marketing, have successfully garnered what is referred to as the "health halo effect"—meaning consumers naturally assume any product with "yogurt" on its label is wholesome and good for you. The only truly healthy yogurt is low-fat plain. If you prefer it sweetened, combine it with some berries or cut up fruit or add a teaspoon or two of maple syrup, honey, or molasses.

2. **Regular Bagels:** The standard bagel is a nutritional disaster—providing a whopping dose of nutrient depleted refined carbs (white flour) that give rise to a truly toxic flash flood of glucose in your arteries. Look for smaller sized, 100 percent whole wheat varieties and spread with a little peanut butter or reduced fat cream cheese to add sensory pleasure and slow down its glycemic response. Your arteries and your waste line will thank you!

3. **Pretzels:** Standard pretzel packages scream "fat-free and natural," but don't be duped. This popular snack food is nothing more than 100 percent refined white flour (that sends your blood glucose straight up!) combined with a whopping dose of sodium. Instead, choose from the growing selection of whole grain or multigrain, crunchy snacks like Multigrain Wheat Thins® or my personal favorite, Food Should Taste Good® whole grain tortilla chips. They provide significantly more fiber and nutrients, and will not spike your blood glucose level like the infamous white flour that pretzels are made from.

4. **Bran muffins:** Unless you make your own, forget these no-icing cupcakes. The standard store-bought (or coffee shop) bran muffin is loaded with white flour, sugar, vegetable oil, additives difficult to pronounce along with a touch of added bran. Don't let that wholesome, rich, brown color fool you. Like colas, it typically comes from added caramel coloring.

5. **Fruit Juice:** Although it can provide some nutrients and a touch of fiber, the standard fruit juiced is loaded with calories and sugar (some have more than soda!). Remember that liquid calories do not suppress your appetite as effectively as solid food calories. It's much better to eat a piece or two of real fruit and drink water instead.

6. **Meal Replacement/Energy Bars:** While some are a bit more wholesome than others, (15 versus 40 or so ingredients) these popular, modern day favorites are the ultimate in 100 percent pure factory made, processed foods. In my book, they are not food, but food-like artifacts that are generally high in sugar and/or unhealthy fats. Have a handful of nuts and a piece of fruit as a real, healthy alternative.

Get Healthy, Save Money

It is my pleasure to share tips for getting healthy that can save you money too. Frankly, there has never been a more opportune time to take charge of your health. Getting healthy can help increase productivity, decrease stress and reduce healthcare costs—all key benefits considering our current economic climate.

Get fit. Regular physical activity remains the single most powerful means to protect broad spectrum health. It is the closest thing we have to the "magic bullet" on the disease prevention and vitality front. Brisk walking is free and perhaps one of the most beneficial types of physical activity.

Make water your beverage of choice. Water has zero calories, costs just a fraction of a cent from the tap (which is where many bottle waters come from) and is the healthiest beverage for the human body. Sodas, fruit drinks, sports drinks, etc., cost money, have minimal to zero nutritionally redeeming value and can lead to weight gain, tooth decay, type 2 diabetes, and metabolic syndrome.

Control your portions! This is a quick and easy way to trim your grocery bill. In fact, recent scientific evidence finds that consistently controlling portions may be the fastest direct route to weight loss.

Prepare your own food. It is cheaper, often quicker, and healthier. People who dine out eat more calories, saturated fat, sugar, and sodium. For a family of four, eating dinner at home even one more time a week can save $100 or more a month.

Buy locally grown produce. It is better for the environment, fresher, tastier, higher in nutrients, and cheaper. Recognize that two-thirds of produce are cheaper in fresh versus frozen form.

Buy produce in bulk. You can save up to 40% by buying large bags of apples or oranges versus purchasing them individually.

Buy staples in volume. There is always better "value in volume"—Examples: 1) A large container of whole oats has 30 servings and costs the same as 10 single serving packets; 2) You can get 12 servings of black beans per bag in dry form versus 3 servings in the can for the same price.

Use non-fat dry milk in baking and cooking. It is dirt cheap and has a long shelf-life.

Stock up on healthy favorites. Fortunately some of the healthiest foods remain the cheapest—Examples: 1) Bags of dried beans have megawatt nutritional power, as they are loaded with fiber, B vitamins, minerals, antioxidants, and healthy vegetable protein and go for about 12 cents per serving. 2) Large bags of brown rice are a delicious and super-nutritious whole grain. You can get a serving for 15 cents.

Go for the specials. Stock up on frozen veggies (no sauces of course) when on sale.

Avoid "convenience" foods—you will always pay more for anything already washed, sliced, or ready-made. Do it yourself to save.

Make a healthy dinner and take leftovers for your lunch the next day.

Have a meatless meal once or twice a week. Beans and rice are an awesome, healthy duo. Veggie stir-fry over brown rice is another one of my family's favorite meatless meals.

Don't shop hungry. You will buy more. Also, leave the kids at home (the "whine" factor works).

Go for the store brands. Most palates can't tell a difference and they are cheaper.

Load up on veggies. Some of the healthiest veggies are often the cheapest, including: cabbage, dark leafy greens, carrots, sweet potatoes, onions, bell peppers, broccoli, cauliflower and tomatoes.

High quality dark chocolate is a truly healthy dessert. You can buy dark chocolate baking chips (ex: Ghiradelli® 60% cacao) and get twice as much for your money versus buying in a bar or individually wrapped pieces.

Make your own salad dressing. Homemade extra virgin olive oil vinaigrette takes three minutes to make, is 100% healthy, and tastes better than the bottled type.

Don't waste your money to purchase bad health. Sodas and standard junk foods, like donuts, cookies, pastries, etc., have zero health value. To the contrary, they can lead to weight gain, type 2 diabetes, heart disease, and a host of other costly conditions. Place value on the nutrients food can provide versus the calories. Most of us are in need of nutrients, not calories. An apple and a pastry cost about the same in the grocery store. Apples are sweet and delicious and provide over 150 health-boosting agents. The pastry provides nothing of value and is actually filled with things that have been associated with poor health, including excess sugar, refined flour, and unhealthy fats.

Eat **Right** For Dessert

If there is one thing that almost all of us have in common, it is a sweet tooth. It would simply be unrealistic to expect any of us to completely forgo dessert. Thankfully, sensible inclusion of the right sweets can fit beautifully into the mix of healthy eating.

Here is a selection of my favorite better-for-you treats to keep you on target tastefully and healthfully.

[THE RIGHT SWEET TOOTH]

High Quality
Dark Chocolate

NUMBER OF SERVINGS
1
NUMBER OF SERVINGS

This delectable, truly healthy dessert has been catapulted to the scientific forefront over the past few years and continues to score one health victory after another. Its accomplishments include boosting brain power, improving insulin sensitivity and improving cardiovascular health. For many, dark chocolate's intense, bittersweet taste means that less chocolate can do the trick. For best results, choose the highest cacao content your palate will accept (strive for at least 60 percent) and limit your indulgence to ⅓ to one ounce. That is about one to two squares from the standard dark chocolate bar found on the grocer shelf. My personal favorite is Lindt® Excellence 85% Cocoa Extra Dark.

Dark Chocolate Is Just The Start Of Healthier Desserts…

Kitchen Tips:
HEALTHIER BAKING

My youngest daughter, Lucie, is aspiring to be the world's best "healthy" chef. She is only in ninth grade and well on her way. She loves to bake and wanted me to share these tips for healthier baking:

➤ Substitute canola oil for shortening, stick margarine or butter. Canola oil/butter blends are also acceptable.

➤ Use ground flax seeds, ground nuts or all natural nut butters in place of bad fats (butter, stick margarine, shortening).

➤ Substitute pureed fruits or starchy veggies (apples, bananas, pears, squash, pumpkin) for some of the oil in your recipes. If a recipe calls for 1 cup oil, use ¾ cup pureed fruit or veggie and ¼ cup oil. Jarred baby foods are great for this purpose.

➤ Replace butter with yogurt.

➤ Substitute whole wheat flour or white whole wheat flour ("Ultra-grain" King Arthur Brand®) for white flour.

➤ Use low-gluten flours (i.e. whole wheat flour, oat flour, brown rice flour)—this reduces the fat content and makes for a more tender product.

➤ Use buttermilk (1% or nonfat) instead of milk or sour cream.

➤ Substitute plain Greek-style yogurt for sour cream.

➤ Substitute dark or semisweet chocolate for milk chocolate.

➤ Substitute pureed dates, honey, maple syrup, or molasses for sugar.

➤ To reduce the fat or butter in your recipes without compromising flavor, add nuts, spices (i.e. cinnamon), instant espresso powder, coffee, cocoa powder, dried fruit, extracts (i.e. vanilla), liqueurs (i.e. amaretto), citrus zests or juice, 100% fruit butters, or nut oils.

➤ To thicken recipes, use gelatin, tapioca, or pectin instead of heavy cream.

➤ To moisten and add nutritional value to baked goods, mix in 100% canned pumpkin or sweet potato puree, grated raw veggies (i.e. carrots), or smashed bananas.

Sip On Some COCOA

Cocoa powder is exploding with super-potent antioxidants called flavanols. Flavanols work all sorts of magic on blood vessels, keeping them open and functioning well. According to a recent clinical trial, enjoying a daily cup of hot cocoa made with skim milk can boost HDL (good cholesterol) and decrease proteins that trigger the development of artery plaque in as little as one month. (*American Journal of Clinical Nutrition*, Nov. 2009) Be sure to use 100% cocoa powder and stay away from the instant varieties.

[THE RIGHT SWEET TOOTH]

Quick Pumpkin Pudding

NUMBER OF SERVINGS • NUMBER OF SERVINGS

1

www.welcoa.org ★ ©2013 Wellness Council of America

This smooth and creamy treat can be prepared instantly and is chock full of nutritional goodness. It is so light in terms of calories and has so much healthy zip that it could also work as a healthy mid-afternoon snack.

Here's how you make this dessert…

Ingredients

1 individual container (about 5.3 oz) of non-fat or low-fat plain Greek yogurt

2–3 tbsp of canned 100% pumpkin

2–3 tsp of molasses

1–2 dash of cinnamon

Directions

Combine ingredients in a small bowl or mug. Stir until thoroughly blended and enjoy.

Dr. Ann's NOTES

➤ As an alternative to the canned 100% pumpkin, you can use canned 100% sweet potatoes. Be careful—don't get the sweet potato pie filling!

➤ I encourage you to test various brands of plain Greek yogurts. They have literally exploded on the grocery scene and are now available in many different brands. The tasting experts at *Cooks Illustrated* magazine recently conducted blind taste tests and "highly recommended" the Olympus® brand. Dannon®, Oikos®, FAGE®, Voskos® and Brown Cow® were also "recommended."

➤ For added texture, feel free to throw in a bit of any of the following: chopped nuts, shredded coconut, dark chocolate chips, diced dried apricots or some of my healthy granola.

[THE RIGHT SWEET TOOTH]

Dr. Ann's
"One Smart Cookie"

I am somewhat obsessed with food and brain function and specifically devised this recipe to capture and exploit the most delicious and robust combination of "brain-boosting" foods that I could fit into a cookie. Yes it has calories and some sugar, but it is loaded with an all-star line up of brain-healthy ingredients. Be **smart** and practice portion control—one cookie is enough!

Here's how you make this dessert…

Ingredients

2 cups old-fashioned oats

1 ½ cups whole wheat flour (I prefer King Arthur White Whole Wheat Flour®)

1 tsp baking soda

½ tsp salt

¼ cup wheat germ

2 tsp cinnamon

⅓ cup canola oil or melted coconut oil

½ cup pureed prunes (I use baby food)

½ cup of molasses (unsulphured is best)

½ cup packed brown sugar

2 large omega-3 eggs

1 tsp vanilla extract

1 cup chopped walnuts

1 ½ cups dark chocolate chips

1 cup dried cranberries (Craisins®)

Directions

Preheat oven to 375 degrees. Combine the dry ingredients (oats, flour, baking soda, salt, cinnamon, wheat germ) in a bowl and mix.

In separate bowl beat oil, sugar, molasses and prune puree until well blended. Beat in the eggs and vanilla. Fold the wet mixture into the dry ingredients and gently mix. Stir in the chocolate chips, walnuts and dried cranberries.

For each cookie, take about 2 heaping tablespoons of dough and form into a ball. Place on a baking sheet covered in pan spray and flatten a bit. Bake until the cookies are golden brown, about 12–14 minutes. Cool on the baking sheet for a few minutes, then transfer to a plate or rack to cool completely. Makes about 24 medium-sized cookies.

Dr. Ann's NOTES

➤ Although I like walnuts in this "brain health" recipe, any nut will work.

➤ Ground flax seed or ground hemp seeds could replace the wheat germ.

➤ I am particularly fond of using molasses in my healthy treats because I love its robust flavor and the fact that it contains many minerals. Along with sugar, you get some magnesium, potassium, calcium, iron, copper and manganese!

[THE RIGHT SWEET TOOTH]

Easy Berry Crisp

NUMBER OF SERVINGS · NUMBER OF SERVINGS

8

Dessert is a regular and revered Sunday night tradition in my home. Each Sunday evening we bake up a yummy, full-fledged treat and this recipe is a unanimous Kulze family favorite. It leverages both the natural sweetness and disease-busting power in berries so you can indulge your sweet tooth with true decadence without compromising your health. It is simply sublime served warm with a scoop of vanilla ice cream.

Here's how you make this dessert…

Ingredients

FILLING

6 cups frozen berries of choice

2 tbsp molasses or granulated sugar (I like Demerara®)

1 tbsp lemon juice

1 tsp cinnamon

¼ tsp salt

¼ cup whole wheat flour

TOPPING

⅔ cup whole wheat flour

⅓ cup old fashioned oats

¼ cup packed brown sugar

¼ cup molasses

¼ cup canola oil or melted coconut oil

⅓ cup chopped pecans or walnuts

½ cup shredded coconut (optional)

Directions

Preheat oven to 375 degrees. Gently toss berries and the remaining filling ingredients together in a medium bowl and mix well. Put the berry filling in an 8 inch square deep baking dish (2 quart) coated with pan spray. Combine the topping ingredients in a medium bowl and stir until well blended. Sprinkle the topping mixture over the fruit and bake at 375 degrees for 30–35 minutes or until the topping has browned and the fruit is bubbling. Serve warm with a scoop of vanilla ice cream (see sidebar for some healthier ice cream options).

Dr. Ann's  NOTES

➤ Feel free to substitute any frozen, unsweetened fruit that you like. Peaches and cherries are delicious too.

➤ Crowning this fruit crisp off with a scoop of ice cream "makes it" as they say. Be vigilant in making your ice cream selections, however. Breyers Smooth & Dreamy®, Edy's Slow Churned Light® and Dreyer's Slow Churned Light® are excellent selections. I also love Purely Decadent Coconut Milk® vanilla "ice cream" because I know that its unique shorter-chained saturated fats are better for my cholesterol profile than dairy-based saturated fats.

[IN SUMMARY]

Cook **Right**, Eat **Right**, Live **Right**

Thank you so much for the opportunity to share my favorite meals, recipes and kitchen wisdom with you and your family. It is my greatest hope that the information in this book will move you beyond the realm of fast food, processed foods and frozen dinners and into your kitchen where you can fully experience the joy, pleasures and vitality that flow from preparing your own meals.

The foods that cross your lips have a profound and lasting impact on every aspect of your health and well-being. And when you start from wholesome, "real food" ingredients as I have shared in this book, nutritional excellence naturally follows. I know with these meal plans and recipes, *Eat Right For Life®: Cookbook Companion* can truly come to life for you and your family just as it has for mine!

As you embark on your kitchen adventures, I would love to hear from you and welcome your feedback at www.DrAnnwellness.com. If you want additional culinary motivation, recipes or menu ideas, each week I post a new "recipe of the week" along with a detailed menu listing of what I served my own family for dinner. Simply go to the "Wellness Resources" tab on my homepage and click "Free Resources." My monthly free enewsletter is also full of helpful tips and advice. For a daily dose of nutrition inspiration you can also follow me on Twitter (DrAnnWellness) and Facebook.

Lastly, I would be grateful if you could share this resource with others. Getting families back to the kitchen table is one of the most powerful avenues available to improve our collective health and well-being.

www.welcoa.org ★ ©2013 Wellness Council of America